Collins Phrase Books

ITALIAN

Collins Phrase Books

FRENCH
GERMAN
ITALIAN
PORTUGUESE
SPANISH
SCANDINAVIAN
RUSSIAN
GREEK
YUGOSLAV
DUTCH

COLLINS PHRASE BOOKS

ITALIAN

Compiled by

Edwin Carpenter
with
John Kelly and Renata Rabassini

COLLINS
LONDON & GLASGOW

First Published 1981
Sixth Reprint 1986

Cover photographs
by courtesy of
Zefa London Ltd.
and Van Phillips

ISBN 0 00 433967 3
© William Collins Sons & Co. Ltd. 1981
Printed in Great Britain
Collins Clear-Type Press

Contents

Introduction 7

FIRST THINGS FIRST
How to Pronounce Italian 8
Everyday Phrases 10
Your First Questions 12
Problems 14
When You Arrive 18

MOVING AROUND
Asking the Way 20
Buses 24
Taxis 25
Trains 26
Service Station 30
Parking 31
Road Conditions 32
Renting a Car 33
Breakdowns & Repairs 34
The Car 36
Accidents & the Police 38

ENJOYING YOUR STAY
Hotels 40
Rented Villas 46
Travelling with a Family 48
Camping 50
Youth Hostels 52
Churches 53
The Weather 54
On the Beach 56
Outdoors & Nightlife 57
Sightseeing 58
Restaurants 60
Menu Reader 64

Contents

Wine List	70
In the Bar	72

SHOPPING
Paying	74
The Basic Phrases	76
Food	78
Newspapers & Stationery	82
Cigarettes	83
The Chemist/Druggist	84
Camera Shop	86
Clothes	88
The Hairdresser	94
Dry Cleaner's & Laundry	96
Repairs	97
The Bank	98
The Post Office	99
Using the Telephone	100

IF YOU'RE ILL
The Doctor	102
The Dentist	107

FOR YOUR INFORMATION
The Time	108
Numbers	110
The Calendar	112
Public Holidays	113
The Alphabet	114
Descriptions	115
Conversion Tables	116
Placenames	118
Signs & Notices	120
Index	122
Personal Details	128

Introduction

For this Phrase Book, we hope we've thought of *almost* everything. If you can't speak Italian, the Collins Italian Phrase Book can help you say what you want whenever you want.

We've thought of what you'll be doing – driving and parking the car, having a drink in a café, buying stamps for your postcards. Each page has a clear heading so you can find your place quickly, and each section contains the phrases you are genuinely likely to need.

We've put ourselves in your shoes and tried to think of the situations that could catch you out. Have you ever been faced with an exotic dish and wanted to know the right way to eat it? or how to ask for a babysitter? These are just the kind of practical questions that you'll find here. And they are in simple but idiomatic Italian, with an easy-to-read pronunciation included.

Besides questions and phrases, we give you the information you need. Many sections begin with a few helpful tips on subjects like using the telephone or travelling by bus. There's a guide to food and wine, so you'll know what to try out, and a full set of conversion tables for everything from tyre pressures to shoe sizes. Bon voyage!

A Word of Advice

This book has been planned to make everything as easy to find as possible, but so that you won't have to fumble when you want a phrase in a hurry, try to read it through before you go away. There's no need to try and learn anything: just remember where the various sections come in the book. It will often be a good idea to look up a key word in the index, and this will take you to what you want to say.

How to Pronounce Italian

We've tried to make the pronunciation helps under the translations as clear as possible. The words have been split up to make them easy to read, but don't hesitate between the syllables. Italian is a fairly easy language to read, and if you listen to the Italians themselves and remember the points made here, you may soon find yourself able to read straight from the translations.

Longer words are usually stressed on the next-to-last syllable, but as we have shown stressed syllables every time, you won't be caught out by the exceptions.

The spellings *c* and *ch* might confuse you, because *c* is sometimes pronounced like English *ch*, while the Italian spelling *ch* is pronounced like English *k*. So *c'è* (there is) is pronounced like English *check* without the final *k* sound, while *che?* (what?) is pronounced *kay*. Also, the spellings *cia*, *cie*, *cio* and *ciu* are pronounced *cha*, *chay*, *cho* and *choo*: the *i* is not pronounced unless it is part of a stressed syllable. The letter *g* behaves in a similar way, as you can see in the table.

The vowels *a*, *e* and *o* can be either 'long' or 'short', that is pronounced as either *a* or *ah*, *e* or *ay*, *o* or *oh*, in different circumstances: you can check in the pronunciations.

Sometimes Italian has two distinct vowel sounds next to each other, in words like *dei*, shown here as **day**-*ee*. These sounds merge into each other, so don't separate them by a long pause.

Finally, be sure to pronounce all the *r's* when you see them in Italian words, and give them a slight trill if you can. In English *r* is often nothing more than a sign to make the vowel sound longer, so that *sore* and *saw* sound the same. Try to pronounce the *r's* as in Scottish English and you should get them right.

Any sound not explained here or on the next page should be clear from the pronunciation help.

How to Pronounce Italian

Italian spelling	Closest English sound	Shown here by	Example	
a	pat	a	quando	**kwan**-doh
	or father	ah	comprare	kom-**prah**-ray
e	pet	e	questo	**kwes**-toh
	or gate	ay	per	payr
i	meet	ee	vino	**vee**-noh
o	UK pot, US thought	o	soldi	**sol**-dee
	or bone	oh	cosa	**koh**-sa
u	boot	oo	luna	**loo**-na
	or won't	w	uomo	**wo**-moh
c	before e, i chat	ch	centro	**chen**-troh
	before a, o, u cat	k	cosa	**koh**-sa
ch	cat	k	che	kay
g	before e, i gin	j or dj	giorno	**jor**-noh
	before a, o, u got	g	regalo	ray-**ga**-loh
gl	million	ly	figlio	**feel**-yoh
gn	companion	ny	bisogno	bee-**zon**-yoh
h	not pronounced		ho	oh
r	carrot, trilled	r	fare	**fah**-ray
s	set	s	soldi	**sol**-dee
	or phase	z	inglese	een-**glay**-zay
sc	before e, i shop	sh	uscita	oo-**shee**-ta
	before a, o, u scar	sk	capisco	ka-**pees**-koh
z	cats	ts	senza	**sent**-sa
	or rods	dz	mezzo	**med**-zoh

Everyday Phrases

To start off, a few phrases you can use for basic contact with the Italian in the street.

Good morning –	Buon giorno *bwon **jor**-noh*
Good afternoon **Good evening** } –	Buona sera *bwoh-na **say**-ra*
Good night –	Buona notte *bwoh-na **not**-tay*
Goodbye –	Arrivederci *ar-ree-ve-**der**-chee*
Yes –	Sì *see*
No –	No *no*
O.K. –	Va bene *va **be**-nay*
How are you? –	Come sta? ***koh**-may sta?*
I'm very well –	Sto bene *Stoh **be**-nay*
Please –	Per favore *per fa-**voh**-ray*
Yes please –	Sì grazie *see **grat**-see-ay*
Thank you –	Grazie ***grat**-see-ay*
No thank you –	No grazie *no **grat**-see-ay*
That's very kind of you –	È molto gentile da parte sua *e **mol**-toh jen-**tee**-lay da **par**-tay **soo**-a*
You're welcome –	Di niente *dee nee-**en**-tay*
I'm sorry –	Mi dispiace *mee dee-spee-**a**-chay*

Everyday Phrases

Excuse me –	Mi scusi *mee **skoo**-see*
It doesn't matter –	Non ha importanza *non a eem-por-**tant**-sa*
I don't mind –	Non importa *non eem-**por**-ta*
My name is Mark Roberts –	Mi chiamo Mark Roberts *mee kee-**a**-moh Mark Roberts*
I come from America –	Vengo dall' America ***ven**-goh dal-la-**may**-ree-ka*
I come from Britain –	Vengo dalla Gran Bretagna ***ven**-goh **dal**-la gran bre-**tan**-ya*
I live in Chester –	Abito a Chester ***a**-bee-toh a Chester*
I am on holiday (vacation) –	Sono in vacanza ***soh**-noh een va-**kant**-sa*
See you soon –	A fra poco *a fra **poh**-koh*

Your First Questions

You won't go very far before you want to ask questions like these.
We may not have given the exact question you need, and you may
have to change a few words, but you should manage. The key part
of some very common questions is in capitals; you can vary the
ending yourself as circumstances require.

I'D LIKE a single room –	VORREI una camera singola *vor-**ray**-ee oo-na **ka**-may-ra **seen**-go-la*
I'D LIKE TO make a phone call –	VORREI fare una telefonata *vor-**ray**-ee **fah**-ray oo-na tay-lay-fo-**na**-ta*
WE WANT TO buy some presents –	VOGLIAMO comprare dei regali *vol-**ya**-moh kom-**prah**-ray **day**-ee ray-**ga**-lee*
How much does that cost? –	Quanto costa quello? ***kwan**-toh **kos**-ta **kwel**-loh?*
I NEED a doctor –	HO BISOGNO DI un medico *oh bee-**zon**-yoh dee oon **me**-dee-koh*
WHERE IS the Tourist Information Office? –	DOV'È l'Ufficio informazioni turistiche? *doh-**ve** loof-**fee**-choh een-for-mat-see-**oh**-nee too-**rees**-tee-kay?*
WE ARE LOOKING FOR a camping site –	CERCHIAMO un campeggio *cher-kee-**a**-moh oon kam-**ped**-joh*
DO YOU KNOW a good restaurant? –	CONOSCE un buon ristorante? *ko-**no**-shay oon bwon rees-to-**ran**-tay?*
SHOULD WE reserve a table? –	È MEGLIO riservare un tavolo? *e **mayl**-yoh ree-ser-**vah**-ray oon **ta**-voh-loh?*
CAN I rent a car? –	POSSO noleggiare una macchina? ***pos**-soh no-led-**jah**-ray oo-na **ma**-kee-na?*
HOW LONG WILL IT TAKE TO repair the car? –	QUANTO TEMPO CI VUOLE PER riparare la macchina? ***kwan**-toh **tem**-poh chee **vwoh**-lay payr ree-pa-**rah**-ray la **ma**-kee-na?*
Can you tell me the time? –	Può dirmi che ore sono? *pwoh **deer**-mee kay **oh**-ray **soh**-noh?*

Your First Questions

WHAT TIME do you close? – A CHE ORA chiudete?
*a kay **oh**-ra kee-oo-**day**-tay?*

WHEN IS THE NEXT TRAIN to Rimini? – QUANDO PARTE IL PROSSIMO TRENO per Rimini?
***kwan**-doh **par**-tay eel **pros**-see-moh **tray**-noh payr **ree**-mee-nee?*

CAN YOU LEND ME a pen? – PUÒ PRESTARMI una penna?
*pwoh pres-**tar**-mee oo-na **pen**-na?*

HAVE YOU GOT any matches? – HA dei fiammiferi?
*a **day**-ee fee-am-**mee**-fay-ree?*

DO I HAVE TIME TO buy a magazine? – HO TEMPO PER comprare una rivista?
*oh **tem**-poh payr kom-**prah**-ray oo-na ree-**vee**-sta?*

What is this? – Che cos'è questo?
*kay **koh**-se **kwes**-toh?*

Who did this? – Chi ha fatto questo?
*kee a **fat**-toh **kwes**-toh?*

Who should I see about this? – A chi dovrei rivolgermi per questo?
*a kee do-**vray**-ee ree-**vol**-jer-mee payr **kwes**-toh?*

Do you mind if I . . .? – Le dispiace se io . . .?
*lay dee-spee-**a**-chay say **ee**-oh . . .?*

Problems

Of course we hope you won't have any, and that if you do they're minor ones and not real emergencies. The phrases we've given here cover both and are meant to help you through any difficulties that may come along.

Can you help me please? – Può aiutarmi per favore?
*pwoh ah-yoo-**tar**-mee payr fa-**voh**-ray?*

Would you come with me please? – Può venire con me per favore?
*pwoh vay-**nee**-ray con may payr fa-**voh**-ray?*

What is the matter? – Che cosa c'è?
*kay **koh**-sa che?*

What do you think is wrong? – Secondo Lei che cosa c'è che non va?
*se-**kon**-doh **lay**-ee kay **koh**-sa che kay non va?*

I don't understand – Non capisco
*non ka-**pees**-koh*

I don't speak Italian – Non parlo italiano
*non **par**-loh ee-ta-lee-**ah**-noh*

Please repeat that – Lo ripeta per favore
*Loh ree-**pay**-ta payr fa-**voh**-ray*

I need someone who speaks English – Ho bisogno di qualcuno che sa parlare inglese
*oh bee-**zon**-yoh dee kwal-**koo**-noh kay sa par-**lah**-ray eeng-**lay**-zay*

I haven't enough money – Non ho abbastanza soldi
*non oh ab-bas-**tant**-sa **sol**-dee*

I have no money – Sono senza soldi
***soh**-noh **sent**-sa **sol**-dee*

Is there somewhere open where we can eat? – C'è qualche posto aperto dove possiamo mangiare?
*che **kwal**-kay **pos**-toh a-**payr**-toh **doh**-vay pos-see-**ah**-moh man-**jah**-ray?*

That man keeps following me – Quell'uomo mi segue
*kwel **wo**-moh mee **say**-gway*

Stop following me – Smetta di seguirmi
***smet**-ta dee say-**gweer**-mee*

Problems

Call the police	Chiamate la polizia *kee-a-mah-tay la po-lit-see-a*
My car has been broken into	Mi hanno rubato dalla macchina *mee an-noh roo-bah-toh dal-la ma-kee-na*
My son is lost	Non trovo più mio figlio *non troh-voh pee-yoo mee-oh feel-yoh*
Where is the police station?	Dov'è la stazione di polizia? *doh-ve la stat-see-oh-nay dee po-lit-see-a?*
I have lost my passport	Ho perso il mio passaporto *oh per-soh eel mee-oh pas-sa-por-toh*
My wallet has been stolen	Mi hanno rubato il portafoglio *me an-noh roo-bah-toh eel-por-ta-fol-yoh*
The insurance company requires me to report it	La compagnia d'assicurazione vuole che la polizia sia informata *la kom-pan-yee-a das-see-koo-rat-see-oh-nay vwoh-lay kay la po-lit-see-a see-a een-for-ma-ta*
I want to see a lawyer	Voglio vedere un avvocato *vol-yoh ve-day-ray oon av-voh-ka-toh*
Please give me my passport back	Per favore restituitemi il mio passaporto *payr fa-voh-ray re-stee-too-ee-tay-mee eel mee-oh pas-sa-por-toh*
Where is the British Consulate?	Dov'è il Consolato Britannico? *doh-ve eel kon-sol-ah-toh bree-tan-nee-koh?*
There is a fire	C'è un incendio *che oon een-chen-dee-oh*
There has been an accident	C'è stato un incidente *che sta-toh oon een-chee-den-tay*
Call an ambulance	Chiamate un'ambulanza *kee-a-mah-tay oon am-boo-lant-sa*
I need a doctor	Ho bisogno di un medico *oh bee-zon-yoh dee oon me-dee-koh*
I feel ill	Mi sento male *mee sen-toh mah-lay*

15

Problems

He has hurt himself	Si è fatto male *see e **fat**-toh **mah**-lay*
My car won't start	La mia macchina non parte *la **mee**-a ma-**kee**-na non **par**-tay*
There is something wrong with the brakes	C'è qualcosa che non va con i freni *che kwal-**koh**-sa kay non va kon ee **fray**-nee*
The machine is broken	La macchina è rotta *la **ma**-kee-na e **rot**-ta*
The air-conditioning does not work	Il condizionatore non funziona *eel kon-deet-see-oh-na-**toh**-ray non foont-see-**oh**-na*
I am in a hurry	Ho fretta *oh **fret**-ta*
How long will this take?	Quanto tempo ci vuole per questo? ***kwan**-toh **tem**-poh chee **vwoh**-lay payr **kwes**-toh?*
How long will the delay be?	Quanto ritardo ci sarà? ***kwan**-toh ree-**tar**-doh chee sa-**ra**?*
I am leaving tomorrow. Can you do it at once?	Parto domani. Può farlo subito? ***par**-toh doh-**mah**-nee. pwoh **far**-loh **soo**-bee-toh?*
I have forgotten my glasses	Ho dimenticato i miei occhiali *oh dee-men-tee-**kah**-toh ee mee-**ay**-ee ok-kee-**ah**-lee*
I have left my bag in the toilet (restroom)	Ho lasciato la mia borsa nella toilette *oh lash-**ah**-toh la **mee**-a **bor**-sa **nel**-la twa-**let***
My luggage has not arrived	I miei bagagli non sono arrivati *ee mee-**ay**-ee ba-**gal**-yee non **soh**-noh ar-ree-**vah**-tee*
I have missed my train	Ho perso il treno *oh **per**-soh eel **tray**-noh*

Problems

The people who were to meet me have not turned up — Le persone che dovevo incontrare non si sono fatte vedere
*lay per-**soh**-nay kay doh-**vay**-voh een-kon-**trah**-ray non see **soh**-noh **fat**-tay ve-**day**-ray*

My party has left without me — Il mio gruppo è partito senza di me
*eel **mee**-oh **groop**-poh e par-**tee**-toh **sent**-sa dee may*

I have lost my way. How do I get to the station? — Ho perso la strada. Come posso arrivare alla stazione?
*oh **per**-soh la **strah**-da. **koh**-may **pos**-soh a-ree-**vah**-ray **al**-la stat-see-oh-**nay**?*

I have broken a glass — Ho rotto un bicchiere
*oh **rot**-toh oon beek-kee-**ay**-ray*

I have spilt something — Ho versato qualcosa
*oh ver-**sah**-toh kwal-**koh**-sa*

My clothes are soaked. Where can I dry them? — I miei vestiti sono bagnati. Dove posso asciugarli?
*ee mee-**ay**-ee ves-**tee**-tee **soh**-noh ban-**yah**-tee. **doh**-vay **pos**-soh a-shoo-**gar**-lee?*

When You Arrive
The Formalities

Entering Italy is usually a simple business. You may possibly be stopped and asked a few questions. The answers given here should be adequate. The two customs channels are red (*oggetti da dichiarare*) for dutiable goods, and green (*niente da dichiarare*) if you have nothing to declare. Check duty-free allowances before you go as they may change from time to time.

Here is my passport – Ecco il mio passaporto
*ek-koh eel **mee**-oh pas-sa-**por**-toh*

My wife and I are on a joint passport – Mia moglie è sul mio passaporto
***mee**-a **mol**-yay e sool **mee**-oh pas-sa-**por**-toh*

Here is my driving licence and green card – Ecco la mia patente e il foglio verde
*ek-koh la **mee**-a pa-**ten**-tay ay eel **fol**-yoh ver-day*

I am staying for 2 weeks – Resto per due settimane
***res**-toh payr **doo**-ay set-tee-**mah**-nay*

I have nothing to declare – Non ho niente da dichiarare
*non oh nee-**en**-tay da dee-kee-a-**rah**-ray*

I have the usual allowances of tobacco and spirits (liquor) – Ho la quantità permessa di tabacco e di alcool
*oh la kwan-tee-**ta** per-**mes**-sa dee ta-**bak**-koh ay dee **al**-koh-ol*

That is for my personal use – Quello è per il mio uso personale
***kwel**-loh e payr eel **mee**-oh **oo**-zoh per-so-**nah**-lay*

How much do I have to pay? – Quanto devo pagare?
***kwan**-toh **day**-voh pa-**gah**-ray?*

Where do I get the connecting flight to Palermo? – Da dove parte il volo di coincidenza per Palermo?
*da **doh**-vay **par**-tay eel **voh**-loh dee koh-een-chee-**dent**-sa payr pa-**ler**-moh?*

Is there a bus into town? – C'è un pullman che va al centro della città?
*che oon **pool**-man kay va al **chen**-troh **del**-la cheet-**ta**?*

When You Arrive
Your Luggage

Where is the luggage from the London flight?	– Dove sono i bagagli del volo da Londra? *doh-vay **soh**-noh ee ba-**gal**-yee del **voh**-loh da **lon**-dra?*
My suitcase is stuck on the conveyor belt	– La mia valigia è incastrata sul nastro ruotante *lan **mee**-a va-**lee**-ja e een-ka-**stra**-ta sool **na**-stroh rwoh-**tan**-tay*
Are there any porters?	– Ci sono dei portabagagli? *chee **soh**-noh **day**-ee por-ta ba-**gal**-yee?*
Are there any luggage trolleys (carriers)?	– Ci sono dei carrelli portabagagli? *chee **soh**-noh **day**-ee kar-**rel**-lee por-ta-ba-**gal**-yee?*
Is there any charge?	– C'è bisogno di pagare? *che bee-**zon**-yoh dee pa-**gah**-ray?*
Is there a left-luggage office (baggage room)?	– C'è un deposito bagagli? *che oon de-**po**-zee-toh ba-**gal**-yee?*
Please take these bags to a taxi	– Per favore porti queste valigie ad un taxi *payr fa-**voh**-ray **por**-tee **kwes**-tay va-**lee**-jay ad oon **tak**-see*
I'll carry that myself	– Porto quello da solo ***por**-toh **kwel**-loh da **soh**-loh*
Careful, the handle is broken	– Attento, il manico è rotto *at-**ten**-toh, eel **ma**-nee-koh e **rot**-toh*
No, don't put that on top	– No, non metta quello in cima *no, non **met**-ta **kwel**-loh een **chee**-ma*
That bag is not mine	– Quella valigia non è mia ***kwel**-la va-**lee**-ja non e **mee**-a*
Where is my other suitcase?	– Dov'è l'altra mia valigia? *doh-**ve lal**-tra **mee**-a va-**lee**-ja?*

Asking the Way
Things you'll hear

It's no use being able to ask the way if you're not going to be able to understand the directions you get. We've tried to anticipate the likely answers, so listen carefully for these key phrases:

Lei va –	**sempre diritto**
lay-ee va	*sem-pray dee-reet-toh*
You go	straight ahead
	– **a destra**
	a des-tra
	right
	– **a sinistra**
	a see-nees-tra
	left
	– **fino a . . .**
	fee-noh a . . .
	as far as . . .
Giri –	**a destra**
jee-ree	*a des-tra*
Turn	right
	– **a sinistra**
	a see-nees-tra
	left
Continui –	**verso . . .**
kon-tee-noo-ee	*ver-soh . . .*
Keep going straight ahead	towards . . .
Segua la segnaletica –	**per . . .**
say-gwa la sen-yal-e-tee-ka	*payr . . .*
Follow the signs	for . . .
Prenda –	**la prima (strada) a destra**
pren-da	*la pree-ma (stra-da) a des-tra*
Take	the first (road) on the right
	– **la seconda (strada) a sinistra**
	la se-kon-da (stra-da) a see-nees-tra
	the second (road) on the left
Bisogna tornare	– You have to turn around
indietro	
bee-zon-ya torr nah-ray	
een-dee-ay-troh	

Asking the Way
Things you'll hear

Attraversi – **la strada**
*at-tra-**ver**-see* *la **stra**-da*
Cross the street

– **la piazza**
*la pee-**at**-sa*
the square

– **al passaggio a livello**
*al pas-**sad**-joh a lee-**vel**-loh*
at the level crossing

È – **all' incrocio**
e *al een-**kroh**-choh*
It's at the junction (intersection)

– **accanto al teatro**
*ak-**kan**-toh al tay-**a**-troh*
next to the theatre

– **dopo il semaforo**
*do-poh eel se-**ma**-fo-roh*
after the traffic lights

– **di fronte alla chiesa**
*dee **fron**-tay **al**-la kee-**ay**-za*
opposite the church

– **lassù**
*las-**soo***
over there

– **dietro l'angolo**
*dee-**e**-troh **lan**-goh-loh*
around the corner

Asking the Way

Where is the cathedral?	Dov'è il duomo? *doh-**ve** eel doo-**oh**-moh?*
Can you tell me the way to the airport?	Può indicarmi la strada per l'aeroporto? *pwo een-dee-**kar**-mee la **stra**-da payr la-ay-ro-**por**-toh?*
Where are the toilets?	Dov'è la toilette? *doh-**ve** la twa-**let**?*
Where is the nearest post office?	Dov'è l'ufficio postale più vicino? *doh-**ve** l'oof-**fee**-choh poh-**sta**-lay pee-**yoo** vee-**chee**-noh?*
Is there a service station near here?	C'è una stazione di servizio qui vicino? *che **oo**-na stat-see-**oh**-nay dee ser-**veet**-see-oh kwee vee-**chee**-noh?*
Is this the right way to the castle?	Va bene questa strada per il castello? *va **bay**-nay **kwes**-ta **stra**-da payr eel kas-**tel**-loh?*
How long will it take to get there?	Quanto tempo ci vuole per arrivarci? ***kwan**-toh **tem**-poh chee **vwoh**-lay payr ar-ree-**var**-chee?*
Is it far?	È lontano? *e lon-**ta**-noh?*
Can you walk there?	Si può andare a piedi? *see pwo an-**dah**-ray a pee-**ay**-dee?*
Is there a bus that goes there?	C'è un pullman che va là? *che oon **pool**-man kay va la?*
Is there a train that goes there?	C'è un treno che va là? *che oon **tray**-noh kay va la?*
Where do I get the bus for Assisi?	Da dove parte il pullman per Assisi? *da **doh**-vay **par**-tay eel **pool**-man payr as-**see**-zee?*
I have lost my way	Ho perso la strada *oh **per**-soh la : **tra**-da*
I am trying to get to the centre of the city	Sto cercando di arrivare in centro *stoh cher-**kan**-doh dee ar-ree-**vah**-ray een **chen**-troh*

I am looking for the Tourist Information Office	Sto cercando l'Ufficio informazioni turistiche *stoh cher-**kan**-doh loof-**fee**-choh een-for-mat-see-**oh**-nee too-**rees**-tee-kay*
Can you show me on the map?	Può mostrarmelo sulla cartina? *pwo mos-**trar**-me-loh **sool**-la kar-**tee**-na?*
Which road do I take for Bologna?	Quale strada devo prendere per Bologna? *kwa-lay **stra**-da **day**-voh **pren**-de-ray payr bo-**lon**-ya?*
How far is it to Venice?	Quanto è distante Venezia? *kwan-toh e dees-**tan**-tay ve-**net**-see-a?*
Will we arrive by this evening?	Arriveremo entro stasera? *ar-ree-ve-**ray**-moh **en**-troh sta-**say**-ra?*
Which is the best route to Perugia?	Qual'è la strada migliore per Perugia? *kwa-**le** la **stra**-da meel-**yoh**-ray payr pe-**roo**-ja?*
Which is the most scenic route?	Qual'è la strada più panoramica? *kwa-**le** la **stra**-da pee-**yoo** pa-no-**ra**-mee-ka?*
Do I turn here for Perugia?	Devo girare qui per Perugia? ***day**-voh jee-**ra**-ray kwee payr pe-**roo**-ja?*
Is the traffic one-way?	È senso unico? *e **sen**-soh **oo**-nee-koh?*
How do I get onto the motorway (highway)?	Come faccio per entrare sull'autostrada? ***ko**-may **fa**-choh payr en-**trah**-ray sool ow-toh-**stra**-da?*
Where does this road go to?	Dove porta questa strada? ***doh**-vay **por**-ta **kwes**-ta **stra**-da?*

Buses

In most cities you'll find a pay-as-you-enter bus system, with a fixed fare for all journeys. Sometimes you can save by buying packs of tickets sold at news stands. Rome, Milan and Naples also have an underground (subway).

Which bus do I take for Piazza Navona?	Quale pullman devo prendere per andare a Piazza Navona? *kwa-lay pool-man day-voh pren-de-ray payr an-dah-ray a pee-at-sa na-voh-na?*
Where do I get a bus for Fiumicino?	Da dove posso prendere un pullman per Fiumicino? *da doh-vay pos-soh pren-de-ray oon pool-man payr fee-oo-mee-chee-noh?*
Does this bus go to the Vatican?	Questo pullman va al Vaticano? *kwes-toh pool-man va al va-tee-ka-noh?*
Where should I change?	Dove devo cambiare? *doh-vay day-voh kam-bee-ah-ray?*
I want to go to the Duomo	Voglio andare al Duomo *vol-yo an-dah-ray al doo-oh-moh*
Where do I buy tickets?	Dove posso comprare dei biglietti? *doh-vay pos-soh kom-prah-ray day-ee beel-yet-tee?*
A pack of bus tickets please	Un blocco di biglietti per il pullman per favore *oon blok-koh dee beel-yet-tee payr eel pool-man payr fa-voh-ray*
Will you let me off at the right stop?	Può dirmi quando devo scendere? *pwo deer-mee kwan-doh day-voh shen-de-ray?*
What is the fare to the centre of the city?	Quanto costa per il centro? *kwan-toh kos-ta payr eel chen-troh?*
When is the last bus?	Quando c'è l'ultimo pullman? *kwan-doh che lool-tee-moh pool-man?*
How long does it take to get to the Vatican?	Quanto tempo ci vuole per arrivare al Vaticano? *kwan-toh tem-poh chee vwoh-lay payr ar-ree-vah-ray al va-tee-ka-noh?*

Taxis

Taxis should be picked up at a stand rather than hailed, and make sure you are taking a real taxi – if it's a pirate cab you may have to pay a lot more than the proper fare.

The main station, please	La stazione principale, per favore *la stat-see-**oh**-nay preen-chee-**pa**-lay payr* *fa-**voh**-ray*
30, Via Roma, please	Via Roma numero trenta, per favore ***vee**-a **roh**-ma **noo**-me-roh **tren**-ta payr* *fa-**voh**-ray*
Please take me to this address	Per favore mi porti a questo indirizzo *payr fa-**voh**-ray mee **por**-tee a **kwes**-toh* *een-dee-**reet**-soh*
Will you put the luggage in the boot (trunk)?	Può mettere i bagagli nel portabagagli? *pwo **met**-te-ray ee ba-**gal**-yee nel* *por-ta-ba-**gal**-yee?*
Please drive us around the town	Per favore ci porti a fare un giro per la città *payr fa-**voh**-ray chee **por**-tee a **fah**-ray oon* *jee-roh payr la cheet-**ta***
I'm in a hurry	Ho fretta *oh **fret**-ta*
Please wait here for a few minutes	Per favore aspetti qui per pochi minuti *payr fa-**voh**-ray as-**pet**-tee kwee payr* ***poh**-kee mee-**noo**-tee*
Turn left please	Giri a sinistra per favore ***jee**-ree a see-**nees**-tra payr fa-**voh**-ray*
Turn right please	Giri a destra per favore ***jee**-ree a **des**-tra payr fa-**voh**-ray*
Please stop at the corner	Per favore si fermi all'angolo *payr fa-**voh**-ray see **fer**-mee al-**lan**-goh-loh*
How much is that please?	Quant'è per favore? *kwan-**te** payr fa-**voh**-ray?*
Keep the change	Tenga il resto ***ten**-ga eel **res**-toh*

Trains
Your Ticket

Travelling by train in Italy is probably more interesting, but slightly more complicated, than at home, and it is a good idea to arrange your journey through a travel agent. You should reserve seats on the crowded summer trains on the main lines, such as Milan – Rome – Naples: in fact you must do so for some de luxe trains. On these and on *rapidi* (express trains) you will also have to pay an extra charge.

Children under ten pay half-fare, and those under four travel free. If you want to travel around you can get a *biglietto chilometrico* which allows you to travel at a reduced rate over a specified distance.

If you travel at night you can reserve a sleeper or a couchette, which is a simple berth with blankets in a compartment shared by several passengers.

A single (one-way ticket) to Rome, please	Uno andata per Roma per favore *oo-noh an-**da**-ta payr **roh**-ma payr fa-**voh**-ray*
A return (round-trip ticket) to Rome, please	Uno andata e ritorno per Roma per favore *oo-noh an-**da**-ta ay ree-**tor**-noh payr **roh**-ma payr fa-**voh**-ray*
A child's return to Rome, please	Uno andata e ritorno ridotto a Roma per favore *oo-noh an-**da**-ta ay ree-**tor**-noh ree-**dot**-toh payr **roh**-ma payr fa-**voh**-ray*
A single to Rome, first class	Uno andata per Roma, prima classe *oo-noh an-**da**-ta payr **roh**-ma, **pree**-ma **klas**-say*
I want to reserve a seat on the 10.30 to Catania	Voglio prenotare un posto sul treno delle dieci e mezza per Catania ***vol**-yoh pray-noh-**tah**-ray oon **pos**-toh sool **tray**-noh **del**-lay dee-e-chee ay **met**-sa payr ka-**ta**-nee-a*

Trains
Your Ticket

Second class, by the window	Seconda classe accanto al finestrino *se-kon-da klas-say ak-kan-toh al* *fee-nes-tree-noh*
A smoking compartment, first class	Scompartimento per fumatori, prima classe *skom-par-tee-men-toh payr' foo-ma-toh-ree,* *pree-ma klas-say*
Can I have a sleeper on the 22.00 to Naples?	Posso avere un posto sul vagone letto delle ventidue per Napoli? *pos-soh a-vay-ray oon pos-toh sool* *va-goh-nay let-toh del-lay ven-tee-doo-ay* *payr na-po-lee?*
Can I have a couchette on the 22.00 to Naples?	Posso avere una cuccetta sul treno delle ventidue per Napoli? *pos-soh a-vay-ray oo-na koo-chet-ta sool* *tray-noh del-lay ven-tee-doo-ay payr* *na-po-lee?*
Can I register (check) my luggage?	Posso registrare i miei bagagli? *pos-soh re-jees-trah-ray ee mee-ay-ee* *ba-gal-yee?*
I want to register (check) these bags	Voglio registrare queste valigie *vol-yoh re-jees-trah-ray kwes-tay* *va-lee-jay*
Where do I pick up my registered luggage?	Dove posso riprendere i miei bagagli registrati? *doh-vay pos-soh ree-pren-de-ray ee* *mee-ay-ee ba-gal-yee re-jees-trah-tee?*
I want to leave these bags in the left luggage (baggage room)	Voglio lasciare queste valigie al deposito bagagli *vol-yoh la-shah-ray kwes-tay va-lee-jay al* *de-po-see-toh ba-gal-yee*
I shall pick them up this evening	Le riprenderò stasera *lay ree-pren-de-roh sta-say-rah*
What time do you close?	A che ora chiude? *a kay oh-ra kee-oo-day?*
How much is it per suitcase?	Quanto costa per valigia? *kwan-toh kos-ta payr va-lee-ja?*

Trains
Boarding the Train

Your ticket will be checked on board the train. Anti-smoking regulations now mean that, as in other public places, smoking is forbidden except in the sections reserved for smokers. On long journeys you can get snacks and hot and cold drinks from attendants who pass through the train or from the platform when the train stops at a station.

Where is the departure board (listing)? – Dov'è la tabella orario?
*doh-ve la ta-**bel**-la oh-**rah**-ree-oh?*

When is the next train to Arezzo? – Quando c'è il prossimo treno per Arezzo?
*kwan-doh che eel **pros**-see-moh **tray**-noh payr a-**ret**-soh?*

What are the times of trains to Arezzo? – Qual'è l'orario dei treni per Arezzo?
*kwa-le loh-**rah**-ree-oh **day**-ee **tray**-nee payr a-**ret**-soh?*

What time is the last train to Arezzo? – Quando parte l'ultimo treno per Arezzo?
*kwan-doh **par**-tay **lool**-tee-moh **tray**-noh payr a-**ret**-soh?*

Please take these bags to platform 9 – Porti queste valigie al binario nove per favore
*por-tee **kwes**-tay va-**lee**-jay al bee-**nah**-ree-oh **noh**-vay payr fa-**voh**-ray*

Would you look after these bags for a minute please? – Potrebbe guardarmi un momento queste valigie per favore?
*po-**treb**-bay gwar-**dar**-mee oon moh-**men**-toh **kwes**-tay va-**lee**-jay payr fa-**voh**-ray?*

What platform do I go to for the Florence train? – A quale binario è il treno per Firenze?
*a **kwa**-lay bee-**nah**-ree-oh e eel **tray**-noh payr fee-**rent**-say?*

Is this the right platform for Florence? – Questo è il binario giusto per Firenze?
*kwes-toh e eel bee-**nah**-ree-oh **joos**-toh payr fee-**rent**-say?*

Trains
In the Train

Is this the Florence train? – È questo il treno per Firenze?
*e **kwes**-toh eel **tray**-noh payr fee-**rent**-say?*

What time does the train leave? – A che ora parte il treno?
*a kay **oh**-ra **par**-tay eel **tray**-noh?*

Is there a dining car? – C'è un vagone ristorante?
*che oon va-**goh**-nay rees-toh-**ran**-tay?*

What time do we get to Verona? – A che ora arriviamo a Verona?
*a kay **oh**-ra ar-ree-vee-**a**-moh a vay-**roh**-na?*

Do we stop at Padua? – Ci fermiamo a Padova?
*chee fayr-mee-**a**-moh a **pa**-doh-va?*

Is this a through train? – Questo è un treno diretto?
***kwes**-toh e oon **tray**-noh dee-**ret**-toh?*

Where do I have to change for Perugia? – Dove devo cambiare per Perugia?
***doh**-vay **day**-voh kam-bee-**ah**-ray payr pe-**roo**-ja?*

Is this seat taken? – Questo posto è occupato?
***kwes**-toh **pos**-toh e ok-koo-**pa**-toh?*

This is my seat – Questo è il mio posto
***kwes**-toh e eel **mee**-oh **pos**-toh*

Can you help me with my bags please? – Mi può aiutare con le valigie per favore?
***mee** pwo a-yoo-**tah**-ray con lay va-**lee**-jay payr fa-**voh**-ray?*

May I open the window? – Posso aprire il finestrino?
***pos**-soh a-**pree**-ray eel fee-nes-**tree**-noh?*

This is a no-smoking compartment – Questo è uno scompartimento per non fumatori
***kwes**-toh e **oon**-oh skom-par-tee-**men**-toh payr non foo-mah-**toh**-ree*

My wife has my ticket – Mia moglie ha il mio biglietto
***mee**-a **mol**-yay a eel **mee**-oh beel-**yet**-toh*

Are we at Bologna yet? – Siamo già a Bologna?
*see-**a**-mo ja a bo-**lon**-ya?*

Are we on time? – Siamo in orario?
*see-**a**-moh een oh-**rah**-ree-oh?*

Driving
Service Station

Benzina, petrol or gas, comes in two varieties in Italy – *normale* (=2 star) and *super* (=4 star). We've set out conversion tables on page 117 for you to work out how many litres to ask for, and to tell you what your metric tyre pressure should be.

15 litres of – **2 star**
Quindici litri di   normale
***kween**-dee-chee **lee**-tree dee*   nor-**ma**-lay

    – **4 star**
    super
    soo-per

    – **diesel fuel**
    gasolio
    *ga-**zol**-yoh*

Fill her up please – Il pieno per favore
*eel **pee**-ay-noh payr fa-**voh**-ray*

Check – **the oil**
Controlli   l'olio
*kon-**trohl**-lee*   *lol-yoh*

    – **the water**
    l'acqua
    lak-wa

    – **the tyre pressure**
    la pressione delle gomme
    *la pres-see-**oh**-nay **del**-lay **gom**-may*

The pressure should be 2.3 – La pressione dovrebbe essere due virgola tre
*la pres-see-**oh**-nay do-**vreb**-bay **es**-se-ray **doo**-ay **veer**-goh-la tray*

I need some distilled water – Ho bisogno di acqua distillata
*oh bee-**zon** yoh dee **ak**-wa dee-steel-**la**-ta*

Could you clean the windscreen (windshield)? – Potrebbe pulire il vetro?
*po-**treb**-bay poo-**lee**-ray eel **ve**-troh?*

Could you put some water in the windscreen washer? – Potrebbe mettere dell'acqua nel serbatoio dei tergicristalli?
*po-**treb**-bay **met**-tuh-ray del-**lak**-wa nel ser-ba-**toy**-oh **day**-ee ter-jee-kree-**stal**-lee?*

Driving
Parking

Although parking meters have begun to appear in Italian cities, most have disc zones, where you leave a parking disc by your windscreen, and this shows when you arrived and when you should leave. There are also supervised parking areas, where it is usual to tip the attendant. Sometimes you will find streets where parking is allowed only on one side on even-numbered dates, and the other side on odd-numbered dates.

Can I park here? – Posso parcheggiare qui?
pos-soh par-ked-jah-ray kwee?

Where is there a car park? – Dov'è un parcheggio?
doh-vay oon par-ked-joh?

Do I need a parking disc? – È necessario il disco orario?
e ne-ches-sah-ree-oh eel dee-skoh oh-rah-ree-oh?

Where can I get a parking disc? – Dove posso trovare un disco orario?
doh-vay pos-soh troh-vah-ray oon dee-skoh oh-rah-ree-oh?

Do I need parking lights? – Devo lasciare accesi i fari di posizione?
day-voh la-shah-ray a-chay-zee ee fah-ree dee po-seet-see-oh-nay?

What time does the car park close? – A che ora chiude il parcheggio?
a kay oh-ra kee-yoo-day eel par-ked-joh?

How long can I stay here? – Per quanto tempo posso stare qui?
payr kwan-toh tem-poh pos-soh stah-ray kwee?

Can I park on this side today? – Posso parcheggiare da questo lato oggi?
pos-soh par-ked-jah-ray da kwes-toh la-toh od-jee?

Driving
Road Conditions

We hope you won't have any problems on Italian roads, but here are a few questions just in case. Remember that you will have to pay a toll for each stretch of the *autostrada* you drive along.

Are there any hold-ups (tie-ups)? – Ci sono dei ritardi?
chee **soh**-*noh* **day**-*ee ree-***tar**-*dee?*

What's causing this hold-up? – Perché c'è questo ritardo?
payr-*kay che* **kwes**-*toh ree-***tar**-*doh?*

Is there a detour? – C'è una deviazione?
che **oo**-*na day-vee-at-see-***oh**-*nay?*

What is the speed limit? – Quanto è il limite di velocità?
kwan-*toh e eel* **lee**-*mee-tay dee ve-lo-chee-***ta**?

Are the roads to Cortina clear? – Le strade per Cortina sono libere?
lay **stra**-*day payr kor-***tee**-*na* **soh**-*noh* **lee**-*be-ray?*

When will the road be clear? – Quando sarà libera la strada?
kwan-*doh sa-***ra** **lee**-*be-ra la* **stra**-*da?*

Is the pass open? – È aperto il valico?
*e a-***payr**-*toh eel* **va**-*lee-koh?*

Is the tunnel open? – È aperta la galleria?
*e a-***payr**-*ta la gal-le-***ree**-*a?*

How much is the toll? – Quanto costa il pedaggio?
kwan-*toh* **kos**-*ta eel pe-***dad**-*joh?*

Driving
Renting a Car

I want to rent a car – Voglio noleggiare una macchina
vol-yoh no-led-jah-ray oo-na ma-kee-na

I want it for 5 days – La voglio per cinque giorni
la vol-yoh payr cheen-kway jor-nee

Is there a charge for mileage? – Bisogna pagare secondo il
chilometraggio?
*bee-zon-ya pa-gah-ray se-kon-doh eel
kee-lo-me-trad-joh?*

Have you got – **a larger car?**
Avete una macchina più grande?
a-vay-tay *oo-na ma-kee-na pee-yoo gran-day?*

– **a cheaper car?**
una macchina più economica?
oo-na ma-kee-na pee-yoo e-ko-no-mee-ka?

– **an automatic?**
una automatica?
oo-na ow-toh-ma-tee-ka?

My wife will be driving as – Anche mia moglie guiderà
well *an-kay mee-a mol-yay gwee-de-ra*

Must I return the car here? – Devo riportare la macchina qui?
*day-voh ree-por-tah-ray la ma-kee-na
kwee?*

I would like to leave the car – Vorrei lasciare la macchina a Rimini
in Rimini *vor-ray-ee la-shah-ray la ma-kee-na a
ree-mee-nee*

Show me how – **the lights work**
Mi faccia vedere come funzionano le luci
mee fa-cha ve-day-ray koh-may *foont-see-oh-na-noh lay loo-chee*

– **the windscreen wipers work**
funzionano i tergicristalli
foont-see-oh-na-noh ee ter-jee-kree-stal-lee

Where is reverse? – Dov'è la marcia indietro?
doh-ve la mar-cha een-dee-e-troh?

Please explain the car – Per favore mi spieghi i documenti di
documents noleggio
*payr fa-voh-ray mee spee-e-gee ee
do-koo-men-tee dee no-layd-joh*

Driving
Breakdowns & Repairs

You should take a red warning triangle with you in case of any breakdowns or accidents.

I have had a breakdown – Sono andato in panne
soh-noh an-da-toh in pan

Can you send – **a mechanic?**
Può mandare   un meccanico?
pwoh man-dah-ray   *oon mek-ka-nee-koh?*

– **a breakdown van (tow-truck)?**
un carro attrezzi?
oon kar-roh at-tret-see?

Can you take me to the – Può portarmi al garage più vicino?
nearest garage?   *pwoh por-tar-mee al ga-raj pee-yoo*
vee-chee-noh?

Can you give me a tow? – Può trainarmi?
pwoh tra-ee-nar-mee?

I have run out of petrol (gas) – Sono senza benzina
soh-noh sent-sa bend-zee-na

Can you give me a can of – Può darmi una tanica di benzina per
petrol, please?   favore?
pwoh dar-mee oo-na ta-nee-ka dee
bend-zee-na payr fa-voh-ray?

There is something wrong – C'è qualcosa che non va nella mia
with my car   macchina
che kwal-koh-sa kay non va nel-la mee-a
ma-kee-na

Can you find the trouble? – Riesce a trovare il problema?
ree-esh-ay a tro-vah-ray eel pro-blay-ma?

I have a flat tyre – Ho una gomma bucata
oh oo-na gom-ma boo-ka-ta

The battery is dead – La batteria è scarica
la bat-te-ree-a e ska-ree-ka

My windscreen (windshield) – Il parabrezza è rotto
has shattered   *eel pa-ra-bred-za e rot-toh*

The engine's overheating – Il motore è surriscaldato
eel moh-toh-ray e soor-ree-skal-da-toh

Driving
Breakdowns & Repairs

There is a leak in the radiator	– Il radiatore perde *eel ra-dee-a-**toh**-ray **payr**-day*
The exhaust pipe has fallen off	– È caduto il tubo di scappamento *e ka-**doo**-toh eel **too**-boh dee skap-pa-**men**-toh*
There is a bad connection	– C'è un contatto difettoso *che oon kon-**tat**-toh dee-fet-**toh**-soh*
I have lost the ignition key	– Ho perso la chiave di accensione *oh **payr**-soh la kee-**ah**-vay dee a-chen-see-**oh**-nay*
I need a new fan belt	– Ho bisogno di una nuova cinghia per il ventilatore *oh bee-**zon**-yoh dee **oo**-na noo-**oh**-va **cheen**-gee-a payr eel ven-tee-la-**toh**-ray*
Can you replace the windscreen wiper?	– Può sostituirmi il tergicristallo? *pwoh sos-tee-too-**eer**-mee eel ter-jee-kree-**stal**-loh?*
Is it serious?	– È una cosa seria? *e **oo**-na **koh**-sa **say**-ree-a?*
How long will it take to repair it?	– Quanto tempo ci vorrà per ripararlo? *kwan-toh **tem**-poh chee vor-**ra** payr ree-pa-**rar**-loh?*
Have you got the parts?	– Avete i pezzi di ricambio? *a-**vay**-tay ee **pet**-see dee ree-**kam**-bee-oh?*
Can you fix it for the time being?	– Può sistemarlo per adesso? *pwoh see-ste-**mar**-loh payr a-**des**-soh?*
Can I have an itemized bill for my insurance company?	– Posso avere un conto dettagliato per la mia compagnia di assicurazione? *pos-soh a-**vay**-ray oon **kon**-toh dayt-tal-ya-toh pay la **mee**-a kom-pan-**yee**-a dee as-see-koo-rat-see-**oh**-nay?*

Driving The Car

accelerator	acceleratore *a-che-le-ra-toh-ray*	**dynamo**	dinamo *dee-na-moh*
air filter	filtro dell'aria *feel-troh del-lah-ree-a*	**electrical system**	impianto elettrico *eem-pee-an-toh e-let-tree-koh*
alternator	alternatore *al-ter-na-toh-ray*	**engine**	motore *moh-toh-ray*
axle	asse *as-say*	**exhaust system**	scappamento *skap-pa-men-toh*
battery	batteria *bat-te-ree-a*	**fan belt**	cinghia del ventilatore *cheen-gee-a del ven-tee-la-toh-ray*
bonnet	cofano *ko-fa-noh*		
boot	portabagagli *por-ta-ba-gal-yee*	**fuel pump**	pompa del carburante *pom-pa del kar-boo-ran-tay*
brakes	freni *fray-nee*		
brake fluid	fluido per i freni *floo-ee-doh payr ee fray-nee*	**fuse**	fusibile *foo-zee-bee-lay*
carburettor	carburatore *kar-boo-ra-toh-ray*	**gear box**	scatola del cambio *ska-toh-la del kam-bee-oh*
choke	valvola dell' aria *val-voh-la del-lah-ree-a*		
clutch	innesto *ee-nes-toh*	**gear lever (shift)**	leva del cambio *lay-va del kam-bee-oh*
cooling system	sistema di raffreddamento *see-stay-ma dee raf-fred-da-men-toh*	**generator**	dinamo *dee-na-moh*
		handbrake	freno a mano *fray-noh a mah-noh*
cylinder	cilindro *chee-leen-droh*	**headlights**	fari anteriori *fah-ree an-tay-ree-oh-ree*
disc brake	freno a disco *frey-noh a dee-skoh*	**heating system**	riscaldamento *ree-skal-da-men-toh*
distributor	distributore *dee-stree-boo-toh-ray*	**hood**	cofano *·ko-fa-noh*

Driving
The Car

hose	manicotto	**spare part**	pezzo di
	*ma-nee-**kot**-toh*		ricambio
indicator	indicatore		*pet-soh dee*
	*een-dee-ka-**toh**-ray*		*ree-**kam**-bee-oh*
jack	cricco	**spark plug**	candela
	***kreek**-koh*		*kan-**day**-la*
lights	fanali	**starter**	motorino
	*fa-**nah**-lee*	**motor**	d'avviamento
muffler	silenziatore		*moh-to-**ree**-noh dav-*
	*see-lent-see-a-**toh**-*		*vee-a-**men**-toh*
	ray	**steering**	sterzo
oil	olio		***stayrt**-soh*
	***ol**-yoh*	**stoplight**	luce indicatrice
oil filter	filtro dell'olio		***loo**-chay*
	***feel**-troh*		*een-dee-ka-**tree**-*
	*del-**lol**-yoh*		*chay*
oil pressure	manometro	**suspension**	sospensione
gauge	dell'olio		*sos-pen-see-**oh**-nay*
	*ma-**no**-me-troh*	**trans-**	trasmissione
	*del-**lol**-yoh*	**mission**	*tras-mees-see-**oh**-*
petrol	benzina		*nay*
	*bend-**zee**-na*	**trunk**	portabagagli
radiator	radiatore		*por-ta-ba-**gal**-yee*
	*ra-dee-a-**toh**-ray*	**turn**	indicatore
rear-view	specchietto	**indicator**	*een-dee-ka-**toh**-ray*
mirror	retrovisore	**tyre**	gomma
	*spek-kee-**et**-toh*		***gom**-ma*
	*re-tro-vee-**zoh**-ray*	**warning**	luce indicatrice
seat	sedile	**light**	***loo**-chay*
	*say-**dee**-lay*		*een-dee-ka-**tree**-*
seat-belt	cintura di		*chay*
	sicurezza	**wheel**	ruota
	*cheen-**too**-ra dee*		*roo-**oh**-ta*
	*see-koo-**ret**-sa*	**windscreen/**	parabrezza
shock	ammortizzatore	**windshield**	*pa-ra-**bred**-za*
absorber	*am-mor-teed-za-*	**wipers**	tergicristalli
	***toh**-ray*		*ter-jee-kree-**stal**-lee*
silencer	silenziatore		
	*see-lent-see-a-**toh**-*		
	ray		

Driving
Accidents & the Police

I'm very sorry, officer –	Mi dispiace molto, signore *mee dee-spee-**a**-chay **mol**-toh seen-**yoh**-ray*
I did not see the signal –	Non ho visto il segnale *non oh **vees**-toh eel sen-**ya**-lay*
I did not know about that regulation –	Non conoscevo quel regolamento *non ko-no-**shay**-voh kwel re-go-la-**men**-toh*
I did not understand the sign –	Non ho capito il segnale stradale *non oh ka-**pee**-toh eel sen-**ya**-lay stra-**da**-lay*
Here is my driving licence –	Ecco la mia patente *ek-koh la **mee**-a pa-**ten**-tay*
Here is my green card –	Ecco la mia carta verde *ek-koh la **mee**-a **kar**-ta **ver**-day*
How much is the fine? –	Quanto è la multa? *kwan-toh e la **mool**-ta?*
I haven't got that much. Can I pay at the police station? –	Non ho quella cifra. Posso pagare alla stazione di polizia? *non oh **kwel**-la **cheef**-ra. **pos**-soh pa-**gah**-ray **al**-la stat-see-**oh**-nay dee po-leet-**see**-a?*
I was driving at 80 kmh –	Stavo guidando ad ottanta *sta-voh gwee-**dan**-doh ad ot-**tan**-ta*
He was too close –	Lui era troppo vicino *loo-ee e-ra **trop**-poh vee-**chee**-noh*
I did not see him –	Non lo avevo visto *non loh a-**vay**-voh **vees**-toh*
He was driving too fast –	Stava guidando troppo forte *sta-va gwee-**dan**-doh **trop**-poh **for**-tay*
He did not stop –	Lui non si è fermato *loo-ee non see e fer-**ma**-toh*
He did not give way (yield) –	Non mi ha dato la precedenza *non mee a **da**-toh la pray-chay-**dent**-sa*
He stopped very suddenly –	Lui si è fermato all'improvviso *loo-ee see a fer-**ma**-toh al-leem-prohv-**vee**-zoh*

Driving
Accidents & the Police

He swerved – Ha scartato
a skar-ta-toh

The car turned without signalling – La macchina ha girato senza mettere le frecce
la ma-kee-na a jee-ra-toh sent-sa met-te-ray lay fre-chay

He ran into me – Mi è venuto addosso
mee e ve-noo-toh ad-dos-soh

He overtook on a bend (passed on a curve) – Ha sorpassato in curva
a sor-pas-sa-toh een koor-va

His car number (licence number) was . . . – Il suo numero di targa era . . .
eel soo-oh noo-me-roh dee tar-ga e-ra . . .

The road was wet – La strada era bagnata
la stra-da e-ra ban-ya-ta

I skidded – Ho sbandato
oh sban-da-toh

My brakes failed – I miei freni non hanno funzionato
ee mee-ay-ee fray-nee non an-noh foont-see-oh-na-toh

I had a blow-out – Ho bucato una gomma
oh boo-ka-toh oo-na gom-ma

I could not stop in time – Non ho potuto fermare in tempo
non oh po-too-toh fer-mah-ray een tem-poh

What is your name and address? – Qual'è il suo nome e indirizzo?
kwa-le eel soo-oh noh-may ay een-dee-reet-soh?

ENJOYING YOUR STAY

Hotels

Hotels are officially graded into categories of 1, 2, 3 or 4 stars and further graded as A, B or C. The accommodation in a boarding house (*pensione*) may also be very good. Many hotels can handle a booking in English, but if you don't want to take any chances . . .

Dear Sirs,
  Egregi Signori,

  I intend to stay in Perugia from 5/6/85 to 9/6/85
    ho intenzione di stare a Perugia dal 5/6/85 al 9/6/85

  – with my wife
    con mia moglie

  – with my family
    con la mia famiglia

  I should be grateful if you could provide the following accommodation:
    Sarei grato se poteste offrirci

  – 1 single room with shower
    una camera singola con doccia

  – 1 room with twin beds and bath
    una camera a due letti con bagno

  – 1 double room (with a bed for a child)
    una camera matrimoniale (con letto aggiunto per un bambino)

  and inform me of your inclusive rates for
    e informarmi dei vostri prezzi complessivi per

  – room and breakfast
    la camera e la colazione

  – room and evening meal
    la mezza pensione

  – room and all meals
    la pensione completa

  I enclose an International Reply coupon
    Allego un 'International Reply Coupon'

Yours faithfully,
  Distinti Saluti,

You'll have to cope with the reply yourself, but if everything is all right it will mention prices; if it begins '*Ci dispiace*', you may have problems. If you're checking in on the spot . . .

My name is . . .	– Mi chiamo . . . *mee kee-**a**-moh . . .*
I reserved a room	– Ho prenotato una camera *oh pray-noh-**ta**-toh **oo**-na **ka**-may-ra*
Do you have a single room?	– Avete una camera singola? *a-**vay**-tay **oo**-na **ka**-may-ra **seen**-go-la?*
Do you have a room with twin beds and shower?	– Avete una camera a due letti con doccia? *a-**vay**-tay **oo**-na **ka**-may-ra a **doo**-ay **let**-tee kon **doh**-cha?*
Do you have a double room with bath?	– Avete una camera matrimoniale con bagno? *a-**vay**-tay **oo**-na **ka**-may-ra ma-tree-moh-nee-**a**-lay kon **ban**-yoh?*
I want to stay for 3 nights	– Voglio restare per tre notti ***vol**-yoh res-**tah**-ray payr tray **not**-tee*
We shall be staying until the sixth of May	– Staremo qui fino al sei maggio *sta-**ray**-moh kwee **fee**-noh al **say**-ee **mad**-joh*
How much is the room per night?	– Quanto costa la camera per una notte? ***kwan**-toh **kos**-ta la **ka**-may-ra payr **oo**-na **not**-tay?*
Is that inclusive?	– Il prezzo comprende tutto? *eel **pret**-so kom-**pren**-day **toot**-toh?*
How much is the room and evening meal?	– Quanto costa la mezza pensione? ***kwan**-toh **kos**-ta la **med**-za pen-see-**oh**-nay?*
How much is the room and all meals?	– Quanto costa la pensione completa? ***kwan**-toh **kos**-ta la pen-see-**oh**-nay kom-**play**-ta?*
Do you have a cot (crib) for our baby?	– Avete un lettino per il nostro bambino? *a-**vay**-tay oon let-**tee**-noh payr eel **nos**-troh bam-**bee**-noh?*

Hotels

What time is – A che ora c'è *a kay **oh**-ra che*	**breakfast?** la colazione? *la ko-lat-see-**oh**-nay?*
	– **lunch?** il pranzo? *eel **prand**-zoh?*
	– **dinner?** la cena? *la **chay**-na?*
Can we have breakfast in our room please?	– Possiamo avere la colazione in camera per favore? *pos-see-**a**-moh a-**vay**-ray la ko-lat-see-**oh**-nay een **ka**-may-ra payr fa-**voh**-ray?*
Where can I park the car?	– Dove posso parcheggiare la macchina? *doh-vay **pos**-soh par-ked-**jah**-ray la **ma**-kee-na?*
What time does the hotel close?	– A che ora chiude l'albergo? *a kay **oh**-ra kee-oo-day lal-**bayr**-goh?*
Is there a lift (elevator)?	– C'è un ascensore? *che oon a-shen-**soh**-ray?*
Can I drink the tap-water?	– L'acqua del rubinetto è potabile? ***lak**-wa del roo-bee-**net**-toh e po-**ta**-bee-lay?*
Please call me at 8 o'clock	– Per favore chiamatemi per le otto *payr fa-**voh**-ray kee-a-**ma**-tay-mee payr lay **ot**-toh*
Can I leave these for safe-keeping?	– Posso lasciare queste cose in custodia? ***pos**-soh la-**sha**-ray **kwes**-tay **koh**-say een koo-**stoh**-dee-a?*
Can I have my things back from the safe?	– Posso avere le cose che avevo lasciato in cassaforte? ***pos**-soh a-**vay**-ray lay **koh**-say kay a-**vay**-voh la-**sha**-toh een kas-sa-**for**-tay?*
Can I make a telephone call from here?	– Posso fare una telefonata da qui? ***pos**-soh **fah**-ray **oo**-na te-le-fo-**na**-ta da kwee?*

Is the voltage 220 or 110? – Il voltaggio è duecentoventi o
centodieci?
*eel vol-**tad**-joh e doo-ay-chen-toh-**ven**-tee oh
chen-toh-dee-**ay**-chee?*

Can I have – **my key please?**
Posso avere   la mia chiave per favore?
***pos**-soh a-**vay**-ray   *la **mee**-a kee-**a**-vay payr fa-**voh**-ray?*

   – **some coat hangers?**
alcuni attaccapanni?
*al-**koo**-nee at-tak-ka-**pan**-nee?*

   – **some note paper?**
dei fogli per scrivere?
***day**-ee fol-yee payr **skree**-ve-ray?*

   – **an ashtray?**
un portacenere?
*oon **por**-ta-**chay**-nay-ray?*

   – **another blanket?**
un'altra coperta?
*oon **al**-tra ko-**payr**-ta?*

   – **another pillow?**
un altro cuscino?
*oon **al**-troh koo-**shee**-noh?*

Where is the socket (outlet) – Dov'è la presa per il mio rasoio?
for my razor?   *doh-**ve** la **pray**-za payr eel **mee**-oh
ra-**zoy**-oh?*

There are no towels in the – Non ci sono asciugamani in camera
room   *non chee **soh**-noh a-shoo-ga-**ma**-nee een
ka-may-ra*

The room is too noisy – C'è troppo rumore in questa camera
*che **trop**-poh roo-**moh**-ray een **kwes**-ta
ka-may-ra*

The light is not working – La luce non funziona
*la **loo**-chay non foont-see-**oh**-na*

The air-conditioning is not – L'aria condizionata non funziona
working   *lah-ree-a kon-deet-see-oh-**na**-ta non
foont-see-**oh**-na*

Hotels

I cannot open the window	Non riesco ad aprire la finestra *non ree-**e**-skoh ad a-**pree**-ray la fee-**nes**-tra*
The heating is not working	Il riscaldamento non funziona *eel ree-skal-da-**men**-toh non foont-see-**oh**-na*
I cannot turn the heating off	Non riesco a spegnere il riscaldamento *non ree-**e**-skoh a **spen**-ye-ray eel ree-skal-da-**men**-toh*
The lock is broken	La serratura è rotta *la ser-ra-**too**-ra e **rot**-ta*
There is no hot water	Non c'è acqua calda *non che **ak**-wa **kal**-da*
The wash basin is dirty	Il lavandino è sporco *eel la-van-**dee**-noh e **spor**-koh*
There is no plug in the wash basin	Non c'è il tappo nel lavandino *non che eel **tap**-poh nel la-van-**dee**-noh*
There is no toilet paper	Non c'è carta igienica *non che **kar**-ta e-je-**nee**-ka*
Do you have a laundry room?	C'è una lavanderia? *che **oo**-na la-van-de-**ree**-a?*
I want to iron some clothes	Voglio stirare alcuni vestiti ***vol**-yoh stee-**rah**-ray al-**koo**-nee ves-**tee**-tee*
I want to stay an extra night	Voglio restare un'altra notte ***vol**-yoh res-**tah**-ray oon **al**-tra **not**-tay*
We will be leaving tomorrow at 9 o'clock	Partiremo domani alle nove *par-tee-**ray**-moh doh-**ma**-nee **al**-lay **noh**-vay*
I would like the bill please	Vorrei avere il conto per favore *vor-**ray**-ee a-**vay**-ray eel **kon**-toh payr fa-**voh**-ray*
Do you accept traveller's cheques?	Accettate dei travellers cheques? *a-chet-**ta**-tay **day**-ee tre-vuh-luhrz shek?*
Could you have my luggage brought down?	Può far portare giù i miei bagagli? *pwoh far por-**tah**-ray joo e mee-**ay**-ee ba-**gal**-yee?*

Can you order me a taxi?	–	Può ordinarmi un taxi?
		pwoh or-dee-__nar__-mee oon __tak__-see?
Thank you. We enjoyed our stay	–	Grazie. Ci siamo trovati bene qui
		__grat__-see-ay. chee see-__a__-moh troh-__va__-tee __be__-nay kwee

If you're a typical absent-minded visitor you might need this letter:

Dear Sirs,
I recently spent some time in your hotel in room 16. I believe I forgot

a pair of shoes

when I left. If you would be good enough to send them on to me I would be most grateful and refund the cost of postage.

Yours faithfully,

Egregi Signori,
recentemente ho trascorso alcuni giorni nel vostro albergo nella stanza numero 16. Credo di aver dimenticato lì

un paio di scarpe

quando sono partito. Se voi poteste spedirmele io vi sarei molto grato e vi rifonderei le spese di spedizione.

Distinti saluti,

Rented Villas

We have arranged to rent a house	Abbiamo deciso di prendere una casa in affitto *ab-bee-**a**-moh day-**chee**-zoh dee* ***pren**-de-ray **oo**-na **ka**-za een af-**feet**-toh*
Here is our booking	Ecco la nostra prenotazione *ek-koh la **nos**-tra pray-noh-tat-see-**oh**-nay*
We need 2 sets of keys	Abbiamo bisogno di due mazzi di chiavi *ab-bee-**a**-moh bee-**zon**-yoh dee **doo**-ay **mat**-see dee kee-**a**-vee*
Will you show us around?	Può farci vedere la casa? *pwoh **far**-chee ve-**day**-ray la **ka**-za?*
Which is the key for this door?	Qual'è la chiave di questa porta? *kwah-**le** la kee-**ah**-vay dee **kwes**-ta **por**-ta?*
Where are the fuses?	Dove sono i fusibili? *doh-vay **soh**-noh ee foo-**zee**-bee-lee?*
Where is the water heater?	Dov'è lo scaldabagno? *doh-**ve** loh skal-da-**ban**-yoh?*
Please show us how this works	Per favore può farci vedere come funziona questo? *payr fa-**voh**-ray pwoh **fahr**-chee ve-**day**-ray **koh**-may foont-see-**oh**-na **kwes**-toh?*
How does the heating work?	Come funziona il riscaldamento? ***koh**-may foont-see-**oh**-na eel ree-skal-da-**men**-toh?*
When does the help come?	Quando viene la donna della pulizia? ***kwan**-doh vee-**ay**-nay la **don**-na **del**-la poo-leet-**see**-a?*
Is there any spare bedding?	C'è altra biancheria per il letto? *che **al**-tra bee-an-ke-**ree**-a payr eel **let**-toh?*
Can I contact you if there are any problems?	Posso mettermi in contatto con voi se ci sono dei problemi? ***pos**-soh **met**-ter-mee een kon-**tat**-toh kon voy say chee **soh**-noh **day**-ee pro-**blay**-mee?*
The cooker (stove) does not work	La cucina non funziona *la coo-**chee**-na non foont-see-**oh**-na*

I can't open the windows – Non riesco ad aprire le finestre
*non ree-**e**-skoh ad a-**pree**-ray lay fee-**nes**-tray*

We can't get any water – Non c'è acqua
*non che **ak**-wa*

The toilet won't flush – Lo sciacquone non funziona
*lo shak-**woh**-nay non foont-see-**oh**-na*

A fuse has blown – È fuso un fusibile
*e **foo**-zoh oon foo-**zee**-bee-lay*

There is a gas leak – C'è una perdita di gas
*che **oo**-na **per**-dee-ta dee gas*

I need somebody to fix this – Ho bisogno di qualcuno per sistemare questo
*oh bee-**zon**-yoh dee kwal-**koo**-noh payr see-ste-**mah**-ray **kwes**-toh*

bath	vasca da bagno *va-ska da ban-yoh*	**pan**	tegame *tay-ga-may*
bathroom	bagno *ban-yoh*	**plate**	piatto *pee-at-toh*
bed	letto *let-toh*	**refrigerator**	frigorifero *free-go-ree-fe-roh*
bottle opener	apribottiglie *a-pree-bot-teel-yay*	**sheet**	lenzuolo *lent-swo-loh*
brush	spazzola *spat-so-la*	**sink**	acquaio *ak-wa-yoh*
can opener	apriscatole *a-pree-ska-toh-lay*	**spoon**	cucchiaio *koo-kee-a-yoh*
chair	sedia *say-dee-a*	**stove**	cucina *koo-chee-na*
cooker	cucina *koo-chee-na*	**table**	tavolo *ta-vo-loh*
corkscrew	cavatappi *ka-va-tap-pee*	**tap**	rubinetto *roo-bee-net-toh*
fork	forchetta *for-ket-ta*	**toilet**	toilette *twa-let*
kitchen	cucina *koo-chee-na*	**vacuum cleaner**	aspirapolvere *as-pee-ra-pol-ve-ray*
knife	coltello *kol-tel-loh*	**wash-basin**	lavandino *la-van-dee-noh*

47

Travelling With A Family

If you take the kids – *i bambini* – away with you, anything can happen and probably will, but these phrases should be useful in at least some of the situations you'll encounter.

There are four of us – Siamo in quattro
*see-**a**-moh een **kwat**-troh*

my wife – mia moglie
***mee**-a **mol**-yay*

my husband – mio marito
***mee**-oh ma-**ree**-toh*

my daughter – mia figlia
***mee**-a **feel**-ya*

my son – mio figlio
***mee**-oh **feel**-yoh*

Have you got a cot (crib) for our baby? – Avete un lettino per il nostro bimbo?
*a-**vay**-tay oon let-**tee**-noh payr eel **nos**-troh **beem**-boh?*

Can my son sleep in our room? – Mio figlio può dormire nella nostra camera?
***mee**-oh **feel**-yoh pwoh dor-**mee**-ray **nel**-la **nos**-tra **ka**-may-ra?*

Are there any other children in the hotel? – Ci sono degli altri bambini in albergo?
*chee **soh**-non **del**-yee **al**-tree bam-**bee**-nee een al-**bayr**-goh?*

How old are your children? – Quanti anni hanno i vostri bambini?
***kwan**-tee **an**-nee **an**-noh ee **vos**-tree bam-**bee**-nee?*

The boy is 9 years old – Il ragazzo ha nove anni
*eel ra-**gat**-soh a **no**-vay **an**-nee*

The girl is 15 months – La bimba ha quindici mesi
*la **beem**-ba a **kween**-dee-chee **may**-zee*

Where can I feed my baby? – Dove posso allattare il mio bambino?
***doh**-vay **pos**-soh al-lat-**tah**-ray eel **mee**-oh bam-**bee**-noh?*

Travelling With A Family

Can you warm this bottle for me?	Può riscaldarmi questo biberon? *pwoh ree-skal-**dar**-mee **kwes**-toh bee-bay-**ron**?*
I need some disposable nappies (diapers)	Ho bisogno di pannolini da buttar via *oh bee-**zon**-yoh dee pan-no-**lee**-nee da **boot**-tar **vee**-a*
Have you got a highchair?	Avete un seggiolone? *a-**vay**-tay oon sed-jo-**loh**-nay?*
Do you know anyone who will babysit for us?	Conosce qualcuno che potrebbe fare da babysitter per noi? *ko-**noh**-shay kwal-**koo**-noh kay po-**treb**-bay **fah**-ray da babysitter payr **no**-ee?*
We will be back at 11	Noi torneremo alle undici *no-ee tor-nay-**ray**-moh **al**-lay **oon**-dee-chee*
She goes to bed at 8	Lei va a letto alle otto *lay-ee va a **let**-toh **al**-lay **ot**-toh*
Are there any organized activities for the children?	Ci sono delle attività organizzate per i bambini? *chee **soh**-noh **del**-lay at-tee-vee-**ta** or-ga-neet-**sa**-tay payr ee bam-**bee**-nee?*
Is there a paddling pool?	C'è una piscina per bambini? *che **oo**-na pee-**shee**-na payr bam-**bee**-nee?*
Is there an amusement park?	C'è un luna park? *che oon **loo**-na park?*
Is there a zoo nearby?	C'è uno zoo qui vicino? *che **oo**-noh tsoh kwee vee-**chee**-noh?*
My son has hurt himself	Mio figlio si è fatto male ***mee**-oh **feel**-yoh see e **fat**-toh **ma**-lay*
My daughter is ill	Mia figlia non sta bene ***mee**-a **feel**-ya non sta **be**-nay*
I'm very sorry – that was very naughty of him	Mi dispiace tanto. È stato molto cattivo *mee dee-spee-**a**-chay **tan**-toh. e **sta**-toh **mol**-toh kat-**tee**-voh*

Camping

Camping in Italy can be a very sophisticated activity, with campers bringing lots of home comforts with them. There are a great number of official camping sites, many with excellent facilities as well as the less comfortable unofficial ones. It generally helps if you have an International Camping Carnet.

Is there anywhere for us to camp near here? – Si può campeggiare qui vicino?
*see pwoh kam-ped-**jah**-ray kwee vee-**chee**-noh?*

Have you a site for our tent? – Avete un posto per la nostra tenda?
*a-**vay**-tay oon **pos**-toh payr la **nos**-tra **ten**-da?*

Do you mind if we camp on your land? – Vi dispiace se campeggiamo sul vostro terreno?
*vee dee-spee-**a**-chay say camp-ped-**ja**-moh sool **vos**-troh ter-**ray**-noh?*

May we pitch our tent here? – Possiamo mettere la tenda qui?
*pos-see-**a**-moh **met**-te-ray la **ten**-da kwee?*

This site is very muddy – Questo posto è molto fangoso
*˜kwes-toh **pos**-toh e **mol**-toh fan-**goh**-soh*

Could we have a more sheltered site? – Possiamo avere un posto più riparato?
*pos-see-**a**-moh a-**vay**-ray oon **pos**-toh pee-**yoo** ree-pa-**ra**-toh?*

Can we put our caravan (trailer) here? – Possiamo mettere la nostra roulotte qui?
*pos-see-**a**-moh **met**-te-ray la **nos**-tra roo-**lot** kwee?*

What facilities are there on the site? – Quali facilitazioni ha questo camping?
*kwa-lee fa-chee-lee-tat-see-**oh**-nee a **kwes**-toh **kam**-ping?*

Is there a shop on the site? – C'è uno spaccio nel camping?
*che **oo**-noh **spa**-choh nel **kam**-ping?*

Can I have a shower? – Posso fare una doccia?
***pos**-soh **fah**-ray **oo**-na **doh**-cha?*

Where is the drinking water? – Dove c'è dell'acqua potabile?
***doh**-vay che del-**lak**-wa po-**ta**-bee-lay?*

50

Camping Equipment

Where are the toilets and washroom?	– Dove sono le toilette e il bagno? *doh-vay soh-noh lay twa-let ay eel ban-yoh?*
Where can we wash our dishes?	– Dove possiamo lavare i piatti? *doh-vay pos-see-a-moh la-vah-ray ee pee-at-tee?*
Is there another camp-site near here?	– C'è un altro camping qui vicino? *che oon al-troh kam-ping kwee vee-chee-noh?*

air-mattress	materassino gonfiabile *ma-tay-ras-see-noh gon-fee-a-bee-lay*	knife	coltello *kol-tel-loh*
back pack	zaino *tsa-ee-noh*	mallet	mazza *mat-sa*
bucket	secchio *sek-kee-oh*	matches	fiammiferi *fee-am-mee-fe-ree*
camp bed	brandina *bran-dee-na*	pail	secchio *sek-kee-oh*
camp chair	seggiolino *sed-jo-lee-noh*	penknife	coltellino *kol-tel-lee-noh*
candle	candela *kan-day-la*	plate	piatto *pee-at-toh*
can opener	apriscatole *a-pree-ska-toh-lay*	rucksack	zaino *tsa-ee-noh*
cup	tazza *tat-sa*	shelter	riparo *ree-pah-roh*
fire	fuoco *foo-oh-koh*	sleeping bag	sacco a pelo *sak-koh a pay-loh*
flashlight	pila *pee-la*	spoon	cucchiaio *kook-kee-a-yoh*
fork	forchetta *for-ket-ta*	tent peg	picchetto *peek-ket-toh*
frying pan	padella *pa-del-la*	tent pole	palo *pa-loh*
ground	terreno *ter-ray-noh*	thermos flask	thermos *ter-mos*
guy line	tirante *tee-ran-tay*	tin opener	apriscatole *a-pree-ska-toh-lay*
		torch	pila *pee-la*

Youth Hostels

Here is my international membership card	– Ecco la mia tessera internazionale *ek-koh la **mee**-a **tes**-say-ra een-ter-nat-see-oh-**na**-lay*
How long can I stay?	– Per quanto tempo posso restare? *payr **kwan**-toh **tem**-poh **pos**-soh res-**tah**-ray?*
I want to stay two nights here	– Voglio stare qui per due notti ***vol**-yoh **stah**-ray kwee payr **doo**-ay **not**-tee*
I would like to join here	– Vorrei iscrivermi qui *vor-**ray**-ee is-**kree**-ver-mee kwee*
Are you open during the day?	– Siete aperti durante il giorno? *see-**ay**-tay a-**payr**-tee doo-**ran**-tay eel **jor**-noh?*
What time do you close?	– A che ora chiudete? *a kay **oh**-ra kee-oo-**day**-tay?*
Do you serve meals?	– Servite dei pasti? *ser-**vee**-tay **day**-ee **pa**-stee?*
Can I use the kitchen?	– Posso usare la cucina? ***pos**-soh oo-**zah**-ray la koo-**chee**-na?*
I want to rent a sheet—sleeping bag	– Voglio noleggiare un sacco lenzuolo ***vol**-yoh no-led-**jah**-ray oon **sak**-koh lent-**swo**-loh*
Is there another youth hostel near here?	– C'è un altro ostello della gioventù qui vicino? *che oon **al**-troh os-**tel**-loh **del**-la jo-ven-**too** kwee vee-**chee**-noh?*

Churches

Where is there – **a Catholic church?**
Dove c'è una chiesa cattolica?
doh-vay che *oo*-na kee-*ay*-za kat-*to*-lee-ka?

– **a Protestant church?**
una chiesa protestante?
oo-na kee-*ay*-za pro-tes-*tan*-tay?

– **a Baptist church?**
una chiesa battista?
oo-na kee-*ay*-za bat-*tees*-ta?

– **a Synagogue?**
una sinagoga?
oo-na see-na-*go*-ga?

– **a Mosque?**
una moschea?
oo-na mo-*skay*-a?

What time is the service? – A che ora c'è il servizio?
*a kay *oh*-ra che eel ser-*veet*-see-oh?*

I'd like to see – **a priest** . . .
Vorrei vedere un prete . . .
*vor-*ray*-ee vay-*day*-ray* *oon *pray*-tay* . . .

– **a minister** . . .
un ministro . . .
*oon mee-*nees*-troh* . . .

– **a rabbi** . . .
un rabbino . . .
*oon rab-*bee*-noh* . . .

. . . who speaks English – . . . che parli inglese
*. . . kay *par-lee* een-*glay*-zay*

What will the choir be singing? – Che cosa canterà il coro?
*kay *koh*-sa kan-te-*ra* eel *koh*-roh?*

The Weather

You may need to know the weather forecast, or you may just wa**n**
to make conversation . . .

It's a lovely day isn't it?	– È una bella giornata, vero? *e **oo**-na **bel**-la jor-**na**-ta, **vay**-roh?*
It's too hot for me	– Fa troppo caldo per me *fa **trop**-poh **kal**-doh payr may*
There's a nice breeze	– C'è un bel venticello *che oon bel ven-tee-**chel**-loh*
It's raining	– Piove *pee-**oh**-vay*
It's windy	– C'è vento *che **ven**-toh*
It's snowing	– Nevica ***ne**-vee-ka*
It's foggy	– C'è la nebbia *che la **neb**-bee-a*
It's cold	– Fa freddo *fa **fred**-doh*
Is it going to be fine?	– Sarà una bella giornata? *sa-**ra oo**-na **bel**-la jor-**na**-ta?*
Is it going to rain?	– Pioverà? *pee-oh-vay-**ra**?*
Is it going to be windy?	– Ci sarà vento? *chee sa-**ra ven**-toh?*
Is it going to snow?	– Nevicherà? *ne-vee-kay-**ra**?*
What is the temperature?	– Quanti gradi ci sono? ***kwan**-tee **gra**-dee chee **soh**-noh?*
Is it going to stay like this?	– Continuerà così? *kon-tee-noo-ay-**ra** koh-**zee**?*
Will the weather improve?	– Il tempo migliorerà? *eel **tem**-poh meel-yoh-ray-**ra**?*
Is it going to get any cooler?	– Farà più fresco? *fa-**ra** pee-**yoo fre**-skoh?*

The Weather

Will the wind go down? – Si calmerà il vento?
*see kal-may-**ra** eel **ven**-toh?*

Is there going to be a thunderstorm? – Ci sarà un temporale?
*chee sa-**ra** oon tem-poh-**ra**-lay?*

Is the sea calm? – È calmo il mare?
*e **kal**-moh eel **mah**-ray?*

Is the water warm? – È calda l'acqua?
*e **kal**-da **lak**-wa?*

When is high tide? – Quando c'è l'alta marea?
***kwan**-doh che **lal**-ta ma-**ray**-a?*

It's a clear night – È una notte chiara
*e **oo**-na **not**-tay kee-**ah**-ra*

Will it be cold tonight? – Farà freddo stasera?
*fa-**ra** **fred**-doh sta-**say**-ra?*

The stars are out – Ci sono le stelle
*chee **soh**-noh lay **stel**-lay*

Leisure & Entertainment
On The Beach

Is it dangerous to swim here? – È pericoloso nuotare qui?
a pe-ree-ko-loh-soh noo-o-tah-ray kwee?

Is this a private beach? – Questa è una spiaggia privata?
kwes-ta e oo-na spee-ad-ja pree-va-ta?

Can you recommend a quiet – Mi può consigliare una spiaggia
beach? tranquilla?
*mee pwoh kon-seel-yah-ray oo-na
spee-ad-ja tran-kweel-la?*

Where can we change? – Dove sono gli spogliatoi?
doh-vay soh-noh lyee spol-ya-toy-ee?

Are there any jelly-fish? – Ci sono delle meduse?
chee soh-noh del-lay me-doo-zay?

Is there a swimming pool? – C'è una piscina?
che oo-na pee-shee-na?

Can I rent – a deck chair?
Posso prendere in affitto una sedia a sdraio?
pos-soh pren-de-ray een *oo-na say-dee-a a zdra-yoh?*
af-feet-toh

– a sunshade?
un ombrellone?
oon om-brel-loh-nay?

– a boat?
una barca?
oo-na bar-ka?

Is it possible to go – sailing?
Si può fare della vela?
see pwoh *fah-ray del-la vay-la?*

– surfing?
fare il surfing?
fah-ray eel sur-fing?

– water-skiing?
fare lo sci d'acqua?
fah-ray lo shee dak-wa?

– skin-diving?
fare la pesca subacquea?
fah-ray la pay-ska soo-bak-way-a?

Leisure & Entertainment
Outdoors & Night Life

Is there somewhere I can – **play tennis?**
C'è qualche posto dove posso   giocare a tennis?
*che **kwal**-kay **pos**-toh **doh**-vay*   *jo-**kah**-ray a ten-nis?*
***pos**-soh*

               – **play golf?**
               giocare a golf?
               *jo-**kah**-ray a golf?*

Is it possible to go riding? – Si può cavalcare?
               *see pwoh ka-val-**kah**-ray?*

Can I go fishing? – Posso andare a pescare?
               ***pos**-soh an-**dah**-ray a pes-**kah**-ray?*

Can I rent the equipment? – Posso noleggiare le attrezzature?
               ***pos**-soh no-led-**jah**-ray lay*
               *at-tret-sa-**too**-ray?*

Is there a football match? – C'è una partita di calcio?
               *che **oo**-na par-**tee**-ta dee **kal**-choh?*

Do you know any interesting – Ci sono delle belle passeggiate?
walks?   *chee **soh**-noh **del**-lay **bel**-lay*
               *pas-sed-**ja**-tay?*

Are there any local festivals? – Ci sono delle feste locali?
               *chee **soh**-noh **del**-lay fes-tay loh-**ka**-lee?*

Are there any films in – Ci sono dei film in inglese?
English?   *chee **soh**-noh **day**-ee feelm een een-**glay**-zay?*

Is there a concert? – C'è un concerto?
               *che oon kon-**cher**-toh?*

2 balcony tickets please – Due biglietti per la galleria per favore
               ***doo**-ay beel-**yet**-tee payr la gal-lay-**ree**-a*
               *payr fa-**voh**-ray*

2 stalls (orchestra) tickets, – Due biglietti per la platea, per favore
please   ***doo**-ay beel-**yet**-tee payr la pla-**tay**-a, payr*
               *fa-**voh**-ray*

Are there any good – Ci sono dei buoni night?
night-clubs?   *chee **soh**-noh **day**-ee boo-**oh**-nee night?*

Is there a disco? – C'è una discoteca?
               *che **oo**-na dee-sko-**tay**-ka?*

Sightseeing

What is there to see here?	– Che c'è da vedere qui? *kay che da vay-**day**-ray kwee?*
Have you got a town guide?	– Ha una guida della città? *ha **oo**-na **gwee**-da **del**-la cheet-**ta**?*
What is this building?	– Che cos'è questo edificio? *kay koh-**ze kwes**-toh ay-dee-**fee**-choh?*
When was it built?	– Quando fu costruito? ***kwan**-doh foo kos-troo-**ee**-toh?*
Is it open to the public?	– È aperto al pubblico? *e a-**payr**-toh al **poob**-blee-koh?*
Are there any sightseeing tours?	– Ci sono delle gite turistiche? *chee **soh**-noh **del**-lay **jee**-tay too-**rees**-tee-kay?*
Is there a tour to the castle?	– C'è una gita al castello? *che **oo**-na **jee**-ta al kas-**tel**-loh?*
Is there a bus tour of the town?	– C'è una gita della città in pullman? *che **oo**-na **jee**-ta **del**-la cheet-**ta** een **pool**-man?*
How long does the tour take?	– Quanto tempo impiega la gita? ***kwan**-toh **tem**-poh eem-pee-**ay**-ga la **jee**-ta?*
Is there a boat trip on the river?	– C'è una gita in barca sul fiume? *che **oo**-na **jee**-ta een **bar**-ka sool fee-**oo**-may?*
Are there any guided tours of the cathedral?	– Ci sono delle gite guidate del duomo? *chee **soh**-noh **del**-lay **jee**-tay goo-ee-**da**-tay del doo-**oh**-moh?*
Is there an English-speaking guide?	– C'è una guida che parla inglese? *che **oo**-na goo-**ee**-da kay **par**-la een-**glay**-zay?*
Have you got an English guide-book?	– Ha una guida scritta in inglese? *a **oo**-na goo-**ee**-da **skreet**-ta een een-**glay**-zay?*
What time does the museum open?	– A che ora apre il museo? *a kay **oh**-ra **a**-pray eel moo-**zay**-oh?*

Can we go in? – Possiamo entrare?
pos-see-a-moh en-trah-ray?

Are these monuments illuminated at night? – Sono illuminati di notte questi monumenti?
soh-noh eel-loo-mee-na-tee dee not-tay kwes-tee mo-noo-men-tee?

Are there any son et lumière displays? – Ci sono degli spettacoli 'son et lumière'?
chee soh-noh del-yee spet-ta-koh-lee 'son et lumière'?

What is the admission charge? – Quanto costa l'ingresso?
kwan-toh kos-ta leen-gres-soh?

Can we go up to the top? – Possiamo andare in cima?
pos-see-a-moh an-dah-ray een chee-ma?

Where is the best view? – Da dove si può vedere il panorama più bello?
da doh-vay see pwoh vay-day-ray eel pa-no-ra-ma pee-yoo bel-loh?

Can I take photos? – Posso fare delle foto?
pos-soh fah-ray del-lay foh-toh?

Can I use a flash? – Posso usare il flash?
pos-soh oo-zah-ray eel flash?

Do you have any postcards? – Avete delle cartoline?
a-vay-tay del-lay kar-to-lee-nay?

Do you have any coloured slides? – Avete delle diapositive?
a-vay-tay del-lay dee-a-po-see-tee-vay?

Where can I buy souvenirs? – Dove posso comprare dei souvenirs?
doh-vay pos-soh kom-prah-ray day-ee soo-ve-neer?

Would you take a photograph of us please? – Potrebbe farci una fotografia per favore?
po-treb-bay far-chee oo-na foh-toh-gra-fee-a payr fa-voh-ray?

Eating & Drinking
Restaurants

A trip to Italy is an invitation to good eating. Even if top-class restaurants are out of your reach, the smaller ones are often memorable and you will often find better food, better service and better prices in a little *trattoria* than in a more pretentious *ristorante*.

Beware of *menu turistici* in places obviously catering for tourists, where the standards are not likely to be high for customers who are only passing through. The best recommendation is the presence of the Italians themselves. The menu-reader on page 64 will help you decide what to eat. Don't miss the opportunity to sample local specialities.

Can we have a table for two?	Possiamo avere un tavolo per due? *pos-see-**a**-moh a-**vay**-ray oon **ta**-vo-loh payr **doo**-ay?*
Can I reserve a table for four at 8 o'clock?	Posso prenotare un tavolo per quattro per le otto? *pos-soh pray-noh-**tah**-ray oon **ta**-vo-loh payr **kwat**-troh payr lay **ot**-toh?*
We'd like a table Vorremmo un tavolo *vor-**raym**-moh oon **ta**-vo-loh*	**by the window** accanto alla finestra *ak-**kan**-toh **al**-la fee-**nes**-tra*
	on the terrace sulla terrazza ***sool**-la ter-**rat**-sa*
The menu please	Il menu per favore *eel me-**noo** payr fa-**voh**-ray*
Do you have a set menu?	Avete un menu fisso? *a-**vay**-tay oon me-**noo** **fees**-soh?*
Is this good?	È buono? *e boo-**oh**-noh?*
What is this dish like?	Com'è questo piatto? ***koh**-me **kwes**-toh pee-**at**-toh?*
What do you recommend?	Che cosa ci consigliate? *kay **koh**-sa chee kon-seel-**ya**-tay?*

Eating & Drinking
Restaurants

Do you have a local speciality?	Avete delle specialità locali? *a-vay-tay del-lay spe-cha-lee-ta loh-ka-lee?*
I'll take that	Prendo quello *pren-doh kwel-loh*
We will begin with spaghetti al pomodoro	Cominceremo con spaghetti al pomodoro *ko-meen-chay-ray-moh kon spa-get-tee al po-mo-do-roh*
I will have steak and chips (French fries)	Voglio una bistecca con patatine fritte *vol-yoh oo-na bee-stayk-ka kon pa-ta-tee-nay freet-tay*
I like it Mi piace *mee pee-a-chay*	**very rare** proprio al sangue *pro-pree-oh al san-gway*
	rare al sangue *al san-gway*
	medium rare poco cotta *poh-koh kot-ta*
	well done cotta bene *kot-ta be-nay*
Are vegetables included?	Comprende anche i contorni? *kom-pren-day an-kay ee kon-tor-nee?*
Is this cheese very strong?	È forte questo formaggio? *e for-tay kwes-toh for-mad-joh?*
That is for me	Questo è per me *kwes-toh e payr may*
That is for over here	Questo è per qui *kwes-toh e payr kwee*
How do I eat this?	Come si mangia questo? *koh-may see man-ja kwes-toh?*
Could we have some more bread please?	Possiamo avere altro pane per favore? *pos-see-a-moh a-vay-ray al-troh pa-nay payr fa-voh-ray?*

Eating & Drinking
Restaurants

Could I have some butter? – Posso avere del burro?
*pos-soh a-**vay**-ray del **boor**-roh?*

What is this called? – Come si chiama questo?
*koh-may see kee-**a**-ma kwes-toh?*

Would you bring another glass please? – Può portare un altro bicchiere per favore?
*pwoh por-**tah**-ray oon **al**-troh beek-kee-e-ray payr fa-**voh**-ray?*

That is not what I ordered – Non ho ordinato questo
*non oh or-dee-**na**-toh **kwes**-toh*

This is very salty – Questo è molto salato
***kwes**-toh e **mol**-toh sa-**la**-toh*

I wanted cheese – Volevo del formaggio
*vo-**lay**-voh del for-**mad**-joh*

Have you forgotten the soup? – Avete dimenticato la minestra?
*a-**vay**-tay dee-men-tee-**ka**-toh la mee-**nes**-tra?*

This is cold – Questo è freddo
***kwes**-toh e **fred**-doh*

This is very good – Questo è molto buono
***kwes**-toh e **mol**-toh boo-**oh**-noh*

I'll have a dessert please – Prenderò il dolce, grazie
*pren-de-**ro** eel **dol**-chay, **grat**-see-ay*

The wine list please – La lista dei vini per favore
*la **lee**-sta **day**-ee **vee**-nee payr fa-**voh**-ray*

Which wine do you recommend? – Quale vino consigliate?
***kwa**-lay **vee**-noh kon-seel-**ya**-tay?*

Is the local wine good? – È buono il vino locale?
*e boo-**oh**-noh eel **vee**-noh loh-**ka**-lay?*

We'll take the Barbera – Prenderemo il Barbera
*pren-de-**ray**-moh eel bar-**bay**-ra*

A small carafe of red wine – Una piccola caraffa di vino rosso
*oo-na **peek**-koh-la ka-**raf**-fa dee **vee**-noh **ros**-soh*

Eating & Drinking
Restaurants

A half-litre bottle of white wine – Un mezzo litro di vino bianco
oon med-zo lee-troh dee vee-noh bee-an-koh

Another bottle please – Un'altra bottiglia per favore
oon al-tra bot-teel-ya payr fa-voh-ray

Some plain water please – Dell'acqua naturale per favore
del-lak-wa na-too-ra-lay payr fa-voh-ray

Some mineral water please – Dell'acqua minerale por favore
del-lak-wa mee-nay-ra-lay payr fa-voh-ray

A beer please – Una birra per favore
oo-na beer-ra payr fa-voh-ray

Black coffee, please – Un caffè per favore
oon kaf-fe payr fa-voh-ray

Coffee with milk, please – Un cappuccino per favore
oon kap-poo-chee-noh payr fa-voh-ray

The bill please – Il conto per favore
eel kon-toh payr fa-voh-ray

We're in a hurry – Abbiamo fretta
ab-bee-a-moh fret-ta

Is service included? – Il servizio è compreso?
eel ser-veet-see-oh e komp-pray-zoh?

There's a mistake here – C'è un errore qui
che oon er-roh-ray kwee

The meal was excellent – Il pasto era eccellente
eel pa-stoh ay-ra e-che-len-tay

Eating & Drinking
Menu Reader

An Italian menu will be divided up into the courses of the meal: hors d'oeuvres are *antipasti*, though *minestre* (literally soups) sometimes appear on menus as well. Other headings are *carne* (meat), *pesce* (fish) and *pasta*. To keep things simple we have listed everything together alphabetically. Many dishes are found everywhere, but Italian cooking is still distinctly regional, so we usually mention the home of the dish.

Acciughe ripiene
Anchovies, with a filling of salted anchovies and cream cheese, fried in oil (Sardinia)

Agnello all'arrabbiata
Roast lamb

Anguille carpionate
Fried eels

Anguille del caldaro
Roasted eels

Anitra in agrodolce
Duck in sweet and sour sauce (Rome)

Aragosta allo spiedo
Spit-roasted lobster (Sardinia)

Arista alla fiorentina
Roast pork loin with herb seasoning (Tuscany)

Asparagi alla parmigiana
Asparagus, boiled, topped with cheese, and baked

Baccalà alla livornese
Salt cod in a tomato sauce (Tuscany)

Baccalà alla vicentina
Salt cod cooked in milk with anchovies, onions, garlic, parsley and herbs (Veneto)

Baccalà mantecato
Salt cod, creamed with milk and olive oil (Veneto)

Bagna calda
Literally a "hot bath", made of olive oil, butter, chopped anchovies and garlic, into which you dip raw vegetables (Piedmont)

Bistecca alla fiorentina
A large charcoal-grilled steak

Bistecca alla pizzaiola
Fried steak in a tomato and herb sauce

Bistecchini di cinghiale
Wild boar steaks (Sardinia)

Brodetto di pesce
Highly seasoned fish soup

Buridda
A fish stew (Liguria, Sardinia)

Calamari in umido
Squid in oil

Calzone
A sort of pizza (Campania)

Caponata
Aubergines (eggplants), peppers, courgettes (zucchini), onions, tomatoes, celery, pine nuts, garlic and herbs, cooked in oil (Sicily)

Eating & Drinking
Menu Reader

Capretto al forno
Roast kid (Abruzzi)

Carciofi alla giudia
Tender artichokes, deep fried (Rome)

Carciofi alla romana
Sautéed stuffed artichokes

Cima alla genovese
Veal with a vegetable and sausage meat stuffing, served cold (Liguria)

Cinghiale alla cacciatora
Wild boar braised in white wine

Cinghiale arrosto
Roast wild boar

Cipolle ripiene
Stuffed onions (Piedmont)

Coniglio in agrodolce
Rabbit in a sweet and sour sauce (Sicily)

Costoletta alla bolognese
Veal cutlet topped with a slice of ham and cheese (Emilia–Romagna)

Costoletta al prosciutto
Veal cutlet with a slice of ham (Emilia–Romagna)

Costolette alla milanese
Veal cutlets in breadcrumbs, fried

Cotechino
Mild pork salami, served hot in slices (Emilia–Romagna)

Cozze fritte
Mussels fried in batter (Apulia)

Crostini di fegatini
Fried bread with chicken liver (Umbria)

Fagioli toscani con tonno
White beans in olive oil with tuna (Tuscany)

Fave al guanciale
Broad beans with onions and bacon

Fegato alla veneziana
Calves' liver and onions (Veneto)

Filetto di tacchino alla bolognese
Turkey breast served with a slice of ham and cheese (Emilia–Romagna)

Fonduta al parmigiano
Slices of *fontina* cheese with a filling of white truffles and grated parmesan, lightly cooked (Emilia–Romagna)

Fritto alla toscana di pollo e funghi
Deep-fried chicken pieces and mushrooms

Fritto misto
Meat, offal, vegetables, fried

Fritto misto alla fiorentina
Various ingredients are used, such as sweetbreads, brains, courgettes (zucchini), coated with batter and deep-fried (Tuscany)

Fritto misto di mare
Mixed fried shellfish

Gnocchi alla fontina
Semolina dumplings, in cheese and breadcrumbs, fried (Piedmont)

Gnocchi al pesto
Little potato dumplings with *pesto*, a cheese and herb mixture (Liguria)

Eating & Drinking
Menu Reader

Gnocchi alla romana
Semolina dumplings with cheese

Gnocchi di mais
Cornflour dumplings topped with tomato sauce and parmesan cheese

Gnocchi verdi
Spinach and cheese dumplings topped with butter and grated cheese (Tuscany)

Involtini
Rolls of veal, with chicken or ham filling, cooked in the oven (Emilia–Romagna)

Lasagne imbottite
A pasta pie with meat and mozzarella cheese (Campania)

Lasagne verdi al forno
Layers of green pasta, filled with meat sauce and white sauce (Emilia–Romagna)

Lepre agrodolce
Hare in a sweet and sour sauce

Lepre alla trentina
Hare cooked in a sweet and sour stock (Trento)

Mazzafegati
Liver sausage (Umbria)

Melanzane alla fiorentina
Aubergines (eggplants), cheese and tomatoes in layers

Melanzane al funghetto
Sautéed aubergines with seasoning

Melanzane alla parmigiana
Aubergines (eggplants) cooked in a sort of pie with mozzarella cheese and tomato sauce and topped with parmesan (Campania)

Melanzane ripiene
Stuffed aubergines

Minestre del paradiso
see Passatelli alla bolognese

Minestrone alla genovese
Vegetable soup flavoured with *pesto*, a cheese and herb mixture (Liguria)

Muggine
Rock mullet (Sardinia)

Osso buco
Shin of veal cooked in wine with tomatoes (Lombardy)

Panzerotti
Fried pasta cushions, with a filling of mozzarella and ham (Apulia)

Pappardelle con la lepre
Wide strips of pasta served in a sauce made from hare (Tuscany)

Passatelli alla bolognese
A mixture of egg, cheese and breadcrumbs, rolled into dumplings, and cooked in stock (Emilia–Romagna)

Pasta alla siciliana
Pasta with a sauce of aubergines (eggplants), tomatoes, red peppers and olives (Sicily)

Pasta alle sarde
Pasta with a sardine sauce (Sicily)

Pasticcio di maccheroni
Macaroni cooked in a sort of pie with a meat sauce, chicken offal and white sauce (Emilia–Romagna)

Eating & Drinking
Menu Reader

Piselli alla toscana
Peas with ham

Piselli al prosciutto
Peas served with onions and ham
(Emilia–Romagna)

Pizza rustica
A pasta pie, with sausage, egg,
cheese and vegetables

Polenta
Maize flour served in various ways

Polenta e osei
Small birds served on *polenta*
(Lombardy)

Polenta pasticciata
Polenta cooked and sliced, with
mushrooms in a white sauce
between the layers (Lombardy)

Pollo alla diavola
Chicken with lemon juice

Pollo alla porchetta
Chicken with ham stuffing

Polpettone
Meat roll of minced veal, ham,
cheese etc

Porchetta
Roast suckling pig

Ragù bolognese
A stew of meat, chicken liver,
tomatoes, garlic (Emilia–
Romagna)

Risi e bisi
A soup with rice and peas in
chicken stock (Veneto)

Riso con tartufi
Rice and truffles (Piedmont)

Risotto alla milanese
Risotto with mushrooms and
cheese

Risotto alla sarda
Risotto with pork, veal and
tomatoes, topped with cheese
(Sardinia)

Risotto con funghi
Risotto with mushrooms

Riso verde
Rice and spinach

Sa cassola
A fish stew (Sardinia)

Salame di felino
A pure pork sausage, lightly
seasoned (Emilia – Romagna)

Saltimbocca
Veal with ham and sage, cooked in
wine (Rome)

Salume
Various types of pork sausages
(Umbria)

Sa merca
Rock mullet (Sardinia)

Sartù di riso
A rice dish with meat, cheese and
vegetables

Scaloppa milanese
Veal escalope in breadcrumbs,
fried

Scaloppine alla perugina
Toast with a topping of chicken
liver and veal

Scampi lessi
Boiled scampi

Eating & Drinking
Menu Reader

Sogliole alla veneziana
Grilled sole

Spaghetti alla carbonara
Spaghetti and chopped bacon;
beaten egg is poured over it to cook
straight away (Rome)

Spaghetti alla matriciana
Spaghetti with a sauce of bacon
and tomatoes (Rome)

Spaghetti alle vongole
Spaghetti with a clam sauce

Spaghetti con cozze
Spaghetti and mussels (Marche)

Stracciatella
Consommé with eggs stirred in to
cook (Rome)

Strecchini alla bolognese
Fried chicken livers, sweetbreads
etc, skewered with slices of cheese,
then cooked in the oven in a white
sauce (Emilia–Romagna)

Strufoli
Little onion- and herb-flavoured
pasties, deep-fried (Friuli)

Supplì
Little balls of cream cheese and
rice, covered in egg and
breadcrumbs and fried

Tacchino stufato al vino bianco
Turkey in white wine

Taccula
Small migrant birds caught and
roasted (Sardinia)

Tagliatelle alla panna
Ribbon-like pasta served in cream
(Emilia–Romagna)

Tonno alla bolognese
Slices of tuna in a vegetable and
white wine sauce (Emilia–
Romagna)

Tortelli alla piacentina
Pasta cushions filled with spinach
and cheese (Emilia – Romagna)

Tortellini alla bolognese
Little coils of egg pasta with a
savoury filling, topped with either
cheese and butter or cream
(Emilia–Romagna)

Trippa alla fiorentina
Tripe in tomato sauce, served with
parmesan (Tuscany)

Trippa alla parmigiana
Tripe with butter and parmesan

Trota alla valdostana
Poached trout in a butter sauce

Vincigrassi
A pie with lasagne and meat in a
smooth sauce (Marche)

Zampone
Stuffed pig's trotter, sliced and
served hot (Emilia–Romagna)

Zuppa di datteri
Shellfish soup (Liguria)

Zuppa di pesce
Fish soup, varies according to the
region

An Italian's meal is usually finished off with cheese or fruit, so we include a list of cheeses and another for those with a fondness for sweet things. Some are bought in pastry-shops rather than restaurants, and *gelati* (ice-cream) are also found in cafés.

Italian Cheeses

Bel paese
Soft, mild cheese from Lombardy

Caciocavallo
A sweetish yellow cheese from the Abruzzi

Fontina
Rather like *gruyère*

Gorgonzola
A tangy blue cheese

Mascarpone
A very creamy cheese, also served as a dessert

Mozzarella
A soft, sweetish cheese

Parmigiano-Reggiano
Otherwise parmesan. Best-known grated in cooking, but this hard cheese is also eaten fresh

Pecorino
Hard, tangy ewe's milk cheese from Umbria

Provolone
A hard tangy cheese from Apulia

Ricotta
A creamy Roman cheese; like Mascarpone it can be served as a dessert

Scamorza
Mozzarella-type cheese, but rather saltier

For the Sweet Tooth

Bucellato
Aniseed-flavoured pastries

Cassata
An ice-cream of different flavours with candied fruit

Granita
A water ice or sherbet

Panforte
Spicy sugar cake

Panettone
A spicy sultana bread

Ricciarelli
Almond biscuits

Scogliatelle
Flaky pastry with cream cheese and fruit (Campania)

Torrone
Nougat

Zabaglione
Egg yolks and sugar whipped till frothy, then Marsala is added

Zuppa inglese
Rather like a trifle, with sponge cake covered with cream

Eating & Drinking
The Wine List

Often it is a good idea to ask for the local wine (*vino locale*). Many of the named Italian wines listed here come in more than one type. They can be red or white (*rosso, bianco*), sweet, semi-sweet or dry (*dolce, abboccato, secco*), sparkling or semi-sparkling (*spumante, frizzante*).

Albanello
White wine, sweet or dry

Aleatico
A red dessert wine

Anghelu rusu
Red dessert wine from Sardinia

Asti
The sparkling Asti Spumante is well-known, but several red and white wines also come from this district

Barbaresco
Dry red wine

Barbera
A good everyday red

Barolo
A solid red

Bianco del collio
White, dry, drunk young

Chianti
The famous red wine in the wicker-covered bottle

Cinqueterre
A dry yellow wine from Liguria

Cirò di Calabria
Medium-dry red

Conegliano
A dry white to be drunk young

Est! Est! Est!
A fine white wine from near Rome.

Frascati
A fine white wine from near Rome. From dry to sweet, depending on the variety

Freisa
A light red, sweet, dry or sparkling

Girò
Dryish red from Sardinia

Lacrima Christi del Vesuvio
A full-bodied red from Campania; there is also a white

Lambrusco
A slightly sparkling red

Malvasia di Lipari
Dessert wine

Marsala
Dark dessert wine from Sicily

Merlot trentino
A good dry red

Montepulciano
A red wine from Tuscany that can be sweet or dry according to age

Moscato
A dessert wine

Nebbiolo
A light red, dry, sweet or sparkling

Eating & Drinking
The Wine List

Orvieto
A sweet or semi-sweet white wine

Pinot
A dry white

Prosecco
Sweet white wine

Sangiovese
A good red

Sangue di Giuda
A sweetish red wine from
Lombardy

Savuto
A dry red wine from Calabria

Soave
Famous dry white from Verona

Tocai del Carso
A dry red Tokay

Tocai del Friuli
A dry white Tokay

Valpolicella
A light red

Verdicchio dei Castelli di Iesi
Dry white from the Marche

Verduzzo
Dry white wine

Vernaccia
Sweet white wine, served as an
aperitif

Vino santo
A white dessert wine

ENJOYING YOUR STAY

In the Bar

Besides selling drinks and giving you the opportunity to enjoy a little local colour, an Italian bar offers some other useful services. In many you will be able to get a snack with your drink; some, called *bar-tabacchi*, have counters selling cigarettes and stamps (phrases on pages 83 and 99). If you see a yellow and black telephone sign outside you can also make calls. Finally, as public toilets are not common in Italy, those in bars serve the purpose. But first you'll want to know how to order.

un bicchiere di vino bianco *oon bee-kee-e-ray dee vee-noh bee-an-koh*	a glass of white wine	**un bicchiere di vino rosso** *oon bee-kee-e-ray dee vee-noh ros-soh*	a glass of red wine
una birra *oo-na beer-ra*	a beer	**un whisky** *oon wis-kee*	a whisky
un brandy *oon bran-dee*	a brandy	**un gin** *oon jeen*	a gin

You might like to try something more typically Italian like a vermouth or an apéritif:

un Cinzano *oon cheent-sa-noh*	**un Martini** *oon mar-tee-nee*
un bitter *oon beet-ter*	**un Campari** *oon kam-pah-ree*

and after dinner:

un marsala *oon mar-sa-la*	**una grappa** *oo-na grap-pa*
un amaro *oon a-mah-roh*	**una sambuca** *oo-na sam-boo-ka*

Marsala is a sweet dessert wine, *grappa* is a kind of brandy, and the others are fruit-based liqueurs. You may want something hot like:

un caffè *oon kaf-fe*	a black coffee	**un tè al latte** *oon te al lat-tay*	tea with milk
un cappuccino *oon kap-poo-chee-noh*	coffee with milk	**un tè al limone** *oon te al lee-moh-nay*	tea with lemon

If you want a soft drink for yourself or the children, you can ask for:

un'aranciata – orangeade
*oo-na-ran-**cha**-ta*
una limonata – fizzy lemon drink
***oon**-na lee-mon-**a**-ta*
una cedrata – limeade
***oon**-na che-**dra**-ta*
un succo di frutta – fruit juice
*oon **sook**-koh dee **froot**-ta*
una spremuta di limone – fresh lemon juice
*oo-na spray-**moo**-ta dee
lee-**moh**-nay*
una spremuta d'arancia – fresh orange juice
*oo-na spray-**moo**-ta da-**ran**-cha*
uno sciroppo di lamponi – raspberry fruit cordial
*oo-noh shee-**rop**-poh dee
lam-**poh**-nee*
uno sciroppo di menta – mint-flavoured cordial
*oo-noh shee-**rop**-poh dee **men**-ta*
uno sciroppo di fragole – strawberry fruit cordial
*oo-noh shee-**rop**-poh dee
fra-goh-lay*

If you feel like a snack, you can pick something from the following selection:

un panino al prosciutto – a ham roll
*oon pa-**nee**-noh al pro-**shoot**-toh*
un panino al formaggio – a cheese roll
*oon pa-**nee**-noh al for-**mad**-joh*
un tramezzino con pasta – an anchovy paste open sandwich
d'acciuga
*oon tra-med-**zee**-noh kon **pas**-ta
da-**choo**-ga*
una brioche – a brioche (a rich bun)
*oo-na bree-**osh**
un toast – a toasted sandwich
oon tohst
una pizzetta – a small slice of pizza
*oo-na peet-**set**-ta*

Paying

These phrases are needed in all sorts of places besides shops, so they have been collected together here.

How much is that?	– Quanto costa quello? *kwan-toh kos-ta kwel-loh?*
I can't afford that much	– Non posso pagare così tanto *non pos-soh pag-ah-ray koh-zee tan-toh*
What does that come to?	– A quanto viene? *a kwan-toh vee-ay-nay?*

How much is it
Quanto costa
kwan-toh kos-ta

– **to get in?**
l'ingresso?
leen-gres-soh?

– **for a child?**
per un bambino?
payr oon bam-bee-noh?

– **to phone to Britain?**
fare una telefonata in Gran Bretagna?
fah-ray oo-na te-lay-fo-na-ta een gran bre-tan-ya?

How much is it
Quanto costa
kwan-toh kos-ta

– **per person?**
a persona?
a per-soh-na?

– **per night?**
per notte?
payr not-tay?

– **per kilo?**
al chilo?
al kee-loh?

– **per metre?**
al metro?
al me-troh?

– **per kilometre?**
al chilometro?
al kee-lo-me-troh?

Is there any extra charge?	– C'è bisogno di pagare un supplemento? *che bee-zon-yoh dee pa-gah-ray oon soop-play-men-toh?*

Paying

Is there any reduction Si fa una riduzione *see fa **oo**-na ree-doot-see-**oh**-nay*	**for a group?** per un gruppo? *payr oon **groop**-poh?*
	for students? per studenti? *payr stoo-**den**-tee?*
	for senior citizens? per cittadini anziani? *payr cheet-ta-**dee**-nee ant-see-**a**-nee?*
Do I pay a deposit?	C'è bisogno di pagare una cauzione? *che bee-**zon**-yoh dee pa-**gah**-ray **oo**-na kowt-see-**oh**-nay?*
Do I pay in advance or afterwards?	Pago in anticipo oppure dopo? *pa-goh een an-**tee**-chee-poh ohp-**poo**-ray do-poh?*
Do you accept traveller's cheques?	Accettate dei traveller's cheques? *a-chet-**ta**-tay day-ee tre-vuh-luhrz shek?*
I want to pay by credit card	Voglio pagare con una carta di credito ***vol**-yoh pa-**gah**-ray kon **oo**-na **kar**-ta dee **kre**-dee-toh*
Can I have a receipt?	Posso avere una ricevuta? ***pos**-soh a-**vay**-ray **oo**-na ree-che-**voo**-ta?*
Can I have an itemized bill?	Posso avere un conto dettagliato? ***pos**-soh a-**vay**-ray oon **kon**-toh det-tal-**ya**-toh?*
I haven't enough money	Non ho abbastanza soldi *non oh ab-ba-**stant**-sa **sol**-dee*
You've given me the wrong change	Il resto è sbagliato *eel **res**-toh e zbal-**ya**-toh*
Please forward it to this address	Per favore inoltratelo a questo indirizzo *payr fa-**voh**-ray ee-nol-**tra**-tay-loh a **kwes**-toh een-dee-**reet**-soh*
Please pack it carefully	Per favore incartatelo con attenzione *payr fa-**voh**-ray een-kar-**ta**-tay-loh kon at-tent-see-**oh**-nay*

The Basic Phrases

Whatever you're buying you'll want phrases like these.

I would like – **a box of matches**
Vorrei   una scatola di fiammiferi
*vor-**ray**-ee*   ***oo**-na **ska**-toh-la dee fee-am-**mee**-fe-ree*

– **some stamps**
dei francobolli
***day**-ee fran-ko-**bol**-lee*

Do you sell sunglasses? – Vendete degli occhiali da sole?
*ven-**day**-tay **del**-yee ok-kee-**a**-lee da **soh**-lay?*

Have you got any – **English newspapers?**
Avete   dei giornali inglesi?
*a-**vay**-tay*   ***day**-ee jor-**na**-lee een-**glay**-zee?*

– **toothpaste?**
del dentifricio?
*del den-tee-**free**-choh?*

I need some suntan oil – Ho bisogno di un olio abbronzante
*oh bee-**zon**-yoh dee oon **ol**-yoh ab-bront-**san**-tay*

Where is – **the shoe department?**
Dov'è   il reparto scarpe?
*doh-**ve***   *eel re-**par**-toh **skar**-pay?*

– **the food department?**
il reparto alimentari?
*eel re-**par**-toh a-lee-men-**tah**-ree?*

Can I see – **the hat in the window?**
Posso vedere   il cappello in vetrina?
***pos**-soh vay-**day**-ray*   *eel kap-**pel**-loh een ve-**tree**-na?*

– **that hat over there?**
quel cappello là?
*kwel keep-**pel**-loh la?*

No, the other one – No, quell'altro
*no, kwel-**lal**-troh*

The Basic Phrases

Have you got – **a larger one?**
Avete   uno più grande?
*a-**vay**-tay*   *oo-noh pee-**yoo gran**-day?*

– **a smaller one?**
uno più piccolo?
*oo-noh pee-**yoo peek**-ko-loh?*

I'm just looking – Sto soltanto guardando
*stoh sol-**tan**-toh gwar-**dan**-doh*

I'm looking for a blouse – Sto cercando una camicetta
*stoh cher-**kan**-doh oo-na ka-mèè-**chet**-ta*

I like this one – Mi piace questo
*mee pee-**a**-chay **kwes**-toh*

I don't like it – Non mi piace
*non mee pee-**a**-chay*

Have you got anything – Avete qualche cosa di più economico?
cheaper?   *a-**vay**-tay **kwal**-kay **koh**-za dee pee-**yoo** ay-ko-**no**-mee-koh?*

I'll take – **this one**
Prenderò   questo
*pren-de-**ro***   ***kwes**-toh*

– **that one**
quello
***kwel**-loh*

– **the other one**
quell'altro
*kwel-**lal**-troh*

Please wrap it – Può incartarlo per favore?
*pwoh een-kar-**tar**-loh payr fa-**voh**-ray?*

There's no need to wrap it – Non c'è bisogno di incartarlo
*non che bee-**zon**-yoh dee een-kar-**tar**-loh*

Can I have a plastic bag? – Posso avere un sacchetto di plastica?
***pos**-soh a-**vay**-ray oon sak-**ket**-toh dee **pla**-stee-ka?*

Food

Of course you can solve all your language problems by heading for the nearest supermarket (*supermercato*), but you will miss the personal touch of the shopkeepers and the people in the market.

I'd like – **a kilo (2 lb.3 oz) of apples**
Vorrei   un chilo di mele
*vor-**ray**-ee*   *oon **kee**-loh dee **may**-lay*

– **a pound (1 lb.1 oz) of tomatoes**
un mezzo chilo di pomodori
*oon **med**-zoh **kee**-loh dee po-mo-**do**-ree*

– **250 gm (9 oz) of butter**
due etti e mezzo di burro
***doo**-ay **et**-tee ay **med**-zoh dee **boor**-roh*

– **100 gm (just under 4 oz) of ground coffee**
un etto di caffè macinato
*oon **et**-toh dee kaf-**fe** ma-chee-**na**-toh*

– **5 slices of ham**
cinque fettine di prosciutto
***cheen**-kway fet-**tee**-nay dee pro-**shoot**-toh*

A bag of sugar, please – Un pacchetto di zucchero, per favore
*oon pak-**ket**-toh dee **tsook**-ke-roh payr fa-**voh**-ray*

A litre of milk, please – Un litro di latte, per favore
*oon **lee**-troh dee **lat**-tay payr fa-**voh**-ray*

A bottle of wine, please – Una bottiglia di vino, per favore
***oo**-na bot-**teel**-ya dee **vee**-noh payr fa-**voh**-ray*

Two pork chops, please – Due braciole di maiale, per favore
***doo**-ay bra-**cho**-lay dee ma-**ya**-lay payr fa-**voh**-ray*

A lamb joint, please – Un pezzo d'agnello, per favore
*oon **pet**-soh dan-**yel**-loh payr fa-**voh**-ray*

A steak, please – Una bistecca, per favore
***oo**-na bee-**stek**-ka payr fa-**voh**-ray*

Food
Meat & Fish

MEAT

beef	manzo *mand-zoh*	**liver**	fegato *fay-ga-toh*
chicken	pollo *pol-loh*	**kidneys**	rognoni *ron-yoh-nee*
ham	prosciutto *pro-shoot-toh*	**pork**	maiale *ma-ya-lay*
lamb	agnello *an-yel-loh*	**veal**	vitello *vee-tel-loh*

FISH

anchovies	acciughe *a-choo-gay*	**mussels**	cozze *cot-say*
clams	vongole *von-goh-lay*	**dentex**	dentice *den-tee-chay*
cod	merluzzo *mer-loot-soh*	**oysters**	ostriche *os-tree-kay*
crab	granchio *gran-kee-oh*	**prawns**	gamberetti *gam-bay-ret-tee*
crayfish	gambero *gam-bay-roh*	**salmon**	salmone *sal-moh-nay*
eels	anguille *an-gweel-lay*	**sardines**	sardine *sar-dee-nay*
hake	nasello *na-zel-loh*	**scampi**	scampi *skam-pee*
halibut	passera *pas-say-ra*	**sole**	sogliola *sol-yoh-la*
herring	aringa *a-reen-ga*	**swordfish**	pesce spada *pe-shay spa-da*
John Dory	pesce san Pietro *pay-shay san pee-ay-troh*	**tench**	tinca *teen-ka*
lobster	aragosta *a-ra-gos-ta*	**trout**	trota *troh-ta*
mackerel	sgombro *zgohm-broh*	**tuna**	tonno *ton-noh*
mullet	triglia *treel-ya*	**whiting**	merlano *mer-la-noh*

79

Food
Groceries & Fruit

GROCERIES

baby food	alimenti per bambini *a-lee-men-tee payr bam-bee-nee*	**margarine**	margarina *mar-ga-ree-na*
biscuits (cookies)	biscotti *bees-kot-tee*	**milk**	latte *lat-tay*
bread	pane *pa-nay*	**mustard**	senape *se-na-pay*
butter	burro *boor-roh*	**oil**	olio *ol-yoh*
cheese	formaggio *for-mad-joh*	**pepper**	pepe *pay-pay*
coffee	caffè *kaf-fe*	**rice**	riso *ree-zoh*
cream	panna *pan-na*	**salt**	sale *sa-lay*
eggs	uova *wo-va*	**soup**	minestra *mee-nes-tra*
flour	farina *fa-ree-na*	**sugar**	zucchero *tsook-ke-roh*
jam	marmellata *mar-mel-la-ta*	**tea**	tè *te*
		vinegar	aceto *a-chay-toh*

FRUIT

apples	mele *may-lay*	**olives**	ulive *oo-lee-vay*
apricots	albicocche *al-bee-kok-kay*	**peaches**	pesche *pes-kay*
bananas	banane *ba-na-nay*	**pears**	pere *pay-ray*
cherries	ciliege *chee-lee-ay-jay*	**pineapple**	ananas *a-na-nas*
grapefruit	pompelmo *pom-pel-moh*	**plums**	susine *soo-zee-nay*
grapes	uva *oo-va*	**pomegranates**	melagrane *may-la-gra-nay*
lemon	limone *lee-moh-nay*	**raspberries**	lamponi *lam-poh-nee*
melon	melone *me-loh-nay*	**strawberries**	fragole *fra-goh-lay*

Food
Vegetables & Herbs

artichoke	carciofo *kar-**cho**-foh*	**marrow**	zucca ***tsook**-ka*
asparagus	asparago *a-**spa**-ra-goh*	**mint**	menta ***men**-ta*
aubergine	melanzana *may-lant-**sa**-na*	**mushroom**	fungo ***foon**-goh*
avocado	avocado *a-vo-**ka**-doh*	**onion**	cipolla *chee-**pohl**-la*
basil	basilico *ba-**zee**-lee-koh*	**parsley**	prezzemolo *pret-**se**-mo-loh*
bay leaf	alloro *al-**lo**-roh*	**parsnip**	pastinaca *pa-stee-**na**-ka*
broad beans	fagiolini *fa-joh-**lee**-nee*	**peas**	piselli *pee-**zel**-lee*
cabbage	cavolo ***ka**-vo-loh*	**potato**	patata *pa-**ta**-ta*
carrot	carota *ka-**ro**-ta*	**radish**	radicchio *ra-**deek**-kee-oh*
cauliflower	cavolfiore *ka-vol-fee-**oh**-ray*	**red pepper**	peperone rosso *pay-pay-**roh**-nay* ***ros**-soh*
celery	sedano ***say**-da-noh*	**rosemary**	rosmarino *rohz-ma-**ree**-noh*
chervil	cerfoglio *cher-**fol**-yo*	**sage**	salvia ***sal**-vee-a*
chicory	cicoria *chee-**koh**-ree-a*	**shallot**	scalogno *ska-**lon**-yoh*
chives	aglio cipollino ***al**-yoh chee-pol- **lee**-noh*	**spinach**	spinaci *spee-**na**-chee*
courgettes	zucchini *tsook-**kee**-nee*	**sweetcorn**	granturco *gran-**toor**-koh*
cucumber	cetriolo *che-tree-**oh**-loh*	**thyme**	timo ***tee**-moh*
garlic	aglio ***al**-yoh*	**tomato**	pomodoro *po-mo-**do**-roh*
green pepper	peperone verde *pay-pay-**roh**-nay* ***ver**-day*	**tarragon**	dragoncello *dra-gon-**chel**-loh*
lettuce	lattuga *lat-**too**-ga*	**zucchini**	zucchini *tsoo-**kee**-nee*

Newspapers & Stationery

If you want a newspaper, you'll get it at a newsstand, *un'edicola*, while stationery is generally sold along with books in a *cartoleria*.

Have you got any	– **English newspapers?**
Avete	dei giornali inglesi?
*a-**vay**-tay*	***day**-ee jor-**na**-lee een-**glay**-zee?*
	– **American newspapers?**
	dei giornali americani?
	***day**-ee jor-**na**-lee a-may-ree-ka-nee?*
	– **postcards?**
	delle cartoline postali?
	***del**-lay kar-toh-**lee**-nay pos-**ta**-lee?*
I would like	– **some notepaper**
Vorrei	dei fogli da lettere
*vor-**ray**-ee*	***day**-ee **fol**-yee da **let**-tay-ray*
	– **some envelopes**
	delle buste
	***del**-lay **boo**-stay*
	– **a pen**
	una penna
	***oo**-na **pen**-na*
	– **a pencil**
	una matita
	***oo**-na ma-**tee**-ta*
I need	– **a bottle of ink**
Ho bisogno di	una bottiglia di inchiostro
*oh bee-**zon**-yoh dee*	***oo**-na bot-**teel**-ya dee een-kee-**os**-troh*
	– **some adhesive tape**
	un nastro adesivo
	*oon **nas**-troh a-day-**zee**-voh*
Do you sell	– **English paperbacks?**
Vendete	dei tascabili inglesi?
*ven-**day**-tay*	***day**-ee tas-**ka**-bee-lee een-**glay**-zee?*
	– **street maps?**
	delle carte stradali?
	***del**-lay **kar**-tay stra-**da**-lee?*
	– **maps of this area?**
	delle carte di questa zona?
	***del**-lay **kar**-tay dee **kwes**-ta **tsoh**-na?*

Cigarettes

Although there are little shops (*tabacchini*) whose main business is selling tobacco, a bar with a cigarette counter is often the easiest place to buy it. British and American brands of cigarettes are often available along with the Italian varieties. Don't forget that wherever tobacco is sold you can also buy stamps; you will find the phrases you want in the Post Office section on page 99.

A packet of . . . please	Un pacchetto di . . . per favore *oon pak-**ket**-toh dee . . . payr fa-**voh**-ray*
with filter-tip	con filtro *kon **feel**-troh*
without filter	senza filtro ***sent**-sa **feel**-troh*
Have you got any American brands?	Avete delle marche americane? *a-**vay**-tay **del**-lay **mar**-kay a-me-ree-**ka**-nay?*
Have you got any English brands?	Avete delle marche inglesi? *a-**vay**-tay **del**-lay **mar**-kay een-**glay**-zee?*
A pipe	Una pipa *oo-na **pee**-pa*
A pouch of pipe tobacco	Un pacchetto di tabacco per pipa *oon pak-**ket**-toh dee ta-**bak**-koh payr **pee**-pa*
Some pipe cleaners	Degli scovolini per la pipa ***del**-yee sko-vo-**lee**-nee payr la **pee**-pa*
A box of matches	Una scatola di fiammiferi *oo-na **ska**-toh-la dee fee-am-**mee**-fe-ree*
A cigar	Un sigaro *oon **see**-ga-roh*
A cigarette lighter	Un accendino *oon a-chen-**dee**-noh*
A gas (butane) refill	Una bomboletta di gas *oo-na bom-boh-**let**-ta dee gas*

The Chemist/Druggist

You should see the *If You're Ill* section if anybody is really unwell, but a chemist should be able to help you with minor ailments. There will be a red cross outside. Some items you usually buy in a chemist at home will not be available – you will have to go to a *profumeria* for cosmetics, and a photographic shop for film.

Can you give me something for a headache? – Può darmi qualche cosa per il mal di testa?
pwoh dar-mee kwal-kay koh-sa payr eel mal dee tes-ta?

I want something for insect bites – Voglio qualche cosa per delle pinzature di insetti
vol-yoh kwal-kay koh-sa payr del-lay pint-sa-too-ray dee een-set-tee

How many do I take? – Quanti ne devo prendere?
kwan-tee nay day-voh pren-de-ray?

How often do I take them? – Quanto spesso dovrei prenderli?
kwan-toh spes-soh dov-ray-ee pren-der-lee?

Is this safe for children? – Va bene per bambini?
va be-nay payr bam-bee-nee?

You might also need something for:

chapped skin	pelle screpolata *pel-lay skre-po-la-ta*	**sunburn**	una scottatura solare *oo-na skot-ta-too-ra soh-lah-ray*
a cold	un raffreddore *oon raf-fred-doh-ray*		
hay fever	febbre da fieno *feb-bray da fee-ay-noh*	**toothache**	il mal di denti *eel mal dee den-tee*
sore feet	piedi dolenti *pee-ay-dee do-len-tee*	**an upset stomach**	il mal di pancia *eel mal'dee pan-cha*
a sore throat	il mal di gola *eel mal dee goh-la*		

or some of the following:

The Chemist/Druggist

aftershave	dopobarba *do-poh-**bar**-ba*	kleenex	kleenex ***klee**-nex*
antihistamine	anti-istaminico *an-tee-ee-sta-**mee**-nee-koh*	lipstick	rossetto *rohs-**set**-to*
antiseptic	antisettico *an-tee-**set**-tee-koh*	mascara	mascara *ma-**skah**-ra*
aspirins	aspirine *a-spee-**ree**-nay*	nail file	limetta *lee-**met**-ta*
bandage	benda ***ben**-da*	nail varnish	smalto ***smal**-toh*
band-aid	cerotto *che-**rot**-toh*	nail varnish remover	solvente *sol-**ven**-tay*
blusher	belletto *bel-**let**-toh*	perfume	profumo *proh-**foo**-moh*
bubble bath	bagno schiuma ***ban**-yoh skee-**oo**-ma*	powder	cipria ***chee**-pree-a*
cleansing milk	latte detergente ***lat**-tay day-ter-**jen**-tay*	razor blades	lamette da barba *la-**met**-tay da **bar**-ba*
contraceptive	contraccettivo *kon-tra-chet-**tee**-voh*	sanitary towels (napkins)	assorbenti *as-sor-**ben**-tee*
cotton wool	cotone idrofilo *ko-**toh**-nay ee-**dro**-fee-loh*	shampoo	shampoo ***sham**-poh*
deodorant	deodorante *day-oh-doh-**ran**-tay*	shaving cream	crema da barba ***kray**-ma da **bar**-ba*
disinfectant	disinfettante *dees-een-fet-**tan**-tay*	skin moisturizer	emolliente per la pelle *ay-mol-lee-**en**-tay payr la-**pel**-lay*
eau de Cologne	acqua di Colonia ***ak**-wa dee ko-**lon**-ee-a*	soap	sapone *sa-**poh**-nay*
eye shadow	rimmel ***reem**-mel*	suntan oil	olio abbronzante ***ol**-yoh ab-brond-**zan**-tay*
hair spray	lacca ***lak**-ka*	talc	talco ***tal**-koh*
hand cream	crema per le mani ***kray**-ma payr lay ma-**nee***	toilet water	acqua di rose ***ak**-wa dee roh-zay*
insect repellent	insettifugo *een-set-tee-**foo**-goh*	toothpaste	dentifricio *den-tee-**free**-choh*

The Camera Shop

I want a film Voglio una pellicola *vol-yoh oo-na pel-lee-koh-la*	**– for this camera** per questa macchina fotografica *payr **kwes**-ta **ma**-kee-na foh-toh-**gra**-fee-ka*
	– for this cine camera per questa cinepresa *payr **kwes**-ta chee-nay-**pray**-za*
	– for black and white prints in bianco e nero *een bee-**an**-koh ay **nay**-roh*
	– for colour prints a colori *a ko-**loh**-ree*
	– for colour slides a colori per diapositive *a ko-**loh**-ree payr dee-a-po-zee-**tee**-vay*
I need batteries for the flash	Ho bisogno di batterie per il flash *oh bee-**zon**-yoh dee bat-tay-**ree**-ay payr eel flash*
Can you develop this film please?	Può sviluppare questa pellicola per favore? *pwoh zvee-loop-**pah**-ray **kwes**-ta pel-**lee**-koh-la payr fa-**voh**-ray?*
I would like 2 prints of this one	Vorrei due copie di questo *vor-**ray**-ee **doo**-ay **kop**-pee-ay dee **kwes**-toh*
When will the photos be ready?	Quando saranno pronte le foto? *kwan-doh sa-**ran**-noh **pron**-tay lay **foh**-toh?*
I would like this photo enlarged	Vorrei un ingrandimento di questa foto *vor-**ray**-ee oon een-gran-dee-**men**-toh dee **kwes**-ta **foh**-toh*
There is something wrong with my camera	C'è qualcosa che non va nella mia macchina fotografica *che kwal-**koh**-sa kay non va **nel**-la **mee**-a **ma**-kee-na foh-toh-**gra**-fee-ka*
The film is jammed	La pellicola è bloccata *la pel-**lee**-koh-la e blok-**ka**-ta*

The Camera Shop
Accessories

accessory	accessorio *a-ches-so-ree-oh*	**over-exposed**	troppo esposto *trop-poh es-pos-toh*
blue filter	filtro blu *feel-troh bloo*	**picture**	fotografia *foh-toh-gra-fee-a*
cassette	cassetta *kas-set-ta*	**projector**	proiettore *pro-yet-toh-ray*
cartridge	caricatore *ka-ree-ka-toh-ray*	**print**	copia *ko-pee-a*
cine-camera	cinepresa *chee-nay-pray-za*	**negative**	negativa *ne-ga-tee-va*
distance	distanza *dee-stant-sa*	**red filter**	filtro rosso *feel-troh ros-soh*
enlargement	ingrandimento *een-gran-dee-men-toh*	**reel**	rotolino *ro-toh-lee-noh*
exposure	tempo di esposizione *tem-poh dee es-poh-zeet-see-oh-nay*	**rewind mechanism**	meccanismo di riavvolgimento *mek-ka-nees-moh dee ree-av-vol-jee-men-toh*
exposure meter	esposimetro *es-po-zee-met-roh*	**shade**	ombra *ohm-bra*
flash	flash *flash*	**slide**	diapositiva *dee-a-po-see-tee-va*
flash bulb	lampadina per il flash *lam-pa-dee-na payr eel flash*	**shutter**	otturatore *ot-too-ra-toh-ray*
		shutter speed	tempo di posa *tem-poh dee poh-za*
flash cube	cubo flash *koo-boh flash*	**transparency**	diapositiva *dee-a-po-see-tee-va*
focal distance	distanza focale *dees-tant-sa foh-ka-lay*	**tripod**	treppiedi *trayp-pee-ay-dee*
focus	fuoco *foo-o-koh*	**under-exposed**	poco esposto *poh-koh es-pos-toh*
in focus	a fuoco *a foo-o-koh*	**view finder**	mirino *mee-ree-noh*
out of focus	non a fuoco *non a foo-o-koh*	**wide-angle lens**	obiettivo grandangolare *o-bee-et-tee-voh gran-dan-goh-lah-ray*
image	immagine *eem-ma-jee-nay*		
lens	obiettivo *o-bee-et-tee-voh*	**yellow filter**	filtro giallo *feel-troh jal-loh*

Clothes
Sizes

First of all you'll want some idea of your continental size. Unfortunately slight variations in sizes mean that these can only be approximate equivalents.

Dresses

UK	10	12	14	16	18
US	8	10	12	14	16
Italy	36	38	40	42	44

Ladies' sweaters

UK/US	32	34	36	38	40
Italy	36	38	40	42	44

Ladies' shoes

UK	3	3½	4	4½	5	5½	6	6½
US	4½	5	5½	6	6½	7	7½	8
Italy	35	36	37	37½	38	38½	39	40

Mens' shoes

UK	7	8	9	10	11
US	8½	9½	10½	11½	12½
Italy	40½	42	43	44	45½

Clothes Sizes

Mens' suits

UK/US	36	38	40	42	44	46
Italy	46	48	50	52	54	56

Waist and chest measurements

inches		28	30	32	34	36	38	40
centimetres		71	76	80	87	91	97	102
inches		42	44	46	48	50	52	54
centimetres		107	112	117	122	127	132	138

Mens' shirts

UK/US	14	14½	15	15½	16	16½	17
Italy	36	37	38	39	41	42	43

Clothes

I would like Vorrei *vor-**ray**-ee*	**– a dress** un vestito *oon ve-**stee**-stoh*
	– a sweater un golf *oon golf*
I take a continental size 40	**– Porto la misura quaranta** ***por**-toh la mee-**zoo**-ra kwa-**ran**-ta*
Can you measure me?	**– Può prendermi le misure?** *pwoh **pren**-der-mee lay mee-**zoo**-ray?*
Have you got something in blue?	**– Avete qualcosa di blu?** *a-**vay**-tay kwal-**koh**-sa dee bloo?*
What is the material?	**– Che stoffa è?** *kay **stof**-fa e?*
I like Mi piace *mee pee-**a**-chay*	**– this one** questo ***kwes**-toh*
	– that one there quello là ***kwel**-loh la*
	– the one in the window quello in vetrina ***kwel**-loh een ve-**tree**-na*
May I take it over to the light?	**– Posso vederlo alla luce?** *pos-soh vay-**dayr**-loh **al**-la **loo**-chay?*
May I try it on?	**– Posso provarlo?** ***pos**-soh proh-**var**-loh?*
Where are the changing rooms?	**– Dove sono i camerini di prova?** ***doh**-vay **soh**-noh ee ka-may-**ree**-nee dee **proh**-va?*
I want a mirror	**– Ho bisogno di uno specchio** *oh bee-**zon**-yoh dee **oo**-noh **spek**-kee-oh*
I like it	**– Mi piace** *mee pee-**a**-chay*

Clothes

I don't like it	Non mi piace
	*non mee pee-**a**-chay*
It doesn't fit properly	Non è la mia misura
	*non e la **mee**-a mee-**zoo**-ra*
It doesn't suit me	Non mi sta bene
	*non mee sta **be**-nay*
I want	**a bigger one**
Ne voglio	uno più grande
*nay **vol**-yoh*	*oo-noh pee-**yoo** gran-day*
	a smaller one
	uno più piccolo
	*oo-noh pee-yoo **peek**-koh-loh*
	one without a belt
	uno senza cintura
	*oo-noh **sent**-sa cheen-**too**-ra*
Is this all you have?	Non ha altro?
	*non a **al**-troh?*
I'll take it	Lo prendo
	*loh **pren**-doh*
Is it washable?	È lavabile?
	*e la-**va**-bee-lay?*
Will it shrink?	Si restringerà?
	*see res-treen-jay-**ra**?*
Must it be dry-cleaned?	Deve essere lavato a secco?
	***day**-vay **es**-se-ray la-**va**-toh a **sek**-koh?*

Clothes

blouse	camicetta *ka-mee-chet-ta*	shorts	pantaloncini *pan-ta-lon-chee-nee*
bra	reggiseno *red-jee-say-noh*	slip	sottoveste *sot-toh-ves-tay*
cardigan	cardigan *kar-dee-gan*	skirt	gonna *gon-na*
coat	cappotto *kap-pot-toh*	sneakers	scarpe da tennis *skar-pay da ten-nis*
dress	vestito *ve-stee-toh*	socks	calzini *kalt-see-nee*
dungarees	pantaloni di fustagno *pan-ta-loh-nee dee foo-stan-yoh*	stockings	calze *kalt-say*
		suit (man's)	vestito *vee-stee-toh*
gloves	guanti *gwan-tee*	suit (woman's)	tailleur *ta-yuhr*
hat	cappello *kap-pel-loh*	sweater	maglione *mal-yoh-nay*
jacket	giacca *jak-ka*	swimsuit	costume da bagno *ko-stoo-may da ban-yoh*
jeans	jeans *jeenz*		
nightdress	camicia da notte *ka-mee-cha da not-tay*	swimming trunks	calzoncini da bagno *kalt-son-chee-nee da ban-yoh*
panties	mutandine *moo-tan-dee-nay*	tie	cravatta *kra-vat-ta*
petticoat	sottoveste *sot-toh-ves-tay*	tights	collant *kol-loñ*
pullover	pullover *pool-loh-ver*	towel	asciugamano *a-shoo-ga-ma-noh*
pyjamas	pigiama *pee-ja-ma*	trousers	pantaloni *pan-ta-loh-nee*
raincoat	impermeabile *eem-payr-mee-a-bee-lay*	T-shirt	maglietta *mal-yet-ta*
		underpants	mutande *moo-tan-day*
sandals	sandali *san-da-lee*	vest	canottiera *ka-not-tee-ay-ra*
shirt	camicia *ka-mee-cha*		

MATERIALS

acrylic	acrilico *a-__kree__-lee-koh*
corduroy	velluto a coste *vel-__loo__-toh a __kos__-tay*
cotton	cotone *ko-__toh__-nay*
denim	tessuto di cotone ritorto *tes-__soo__-toh dee ko-__toh__-nay ree-__tor__-toh*
fur	pelliccia *pel-__lee__-cha*
jersey	jersey *__jer__-sey*
lace	pizzo *__peet__-soh*
leather	cuoio *koo-__oy__-oh*
linen	lino *__lee__-noh*
nylon	nylon *__nye__-lon*
polyester	poliestere *pol-lee-__es__-te-ray*
poplin	popeline *po-pe-__leen__*
rayon	raion *__ra__-yon*
silk	seta *__say__-ta*
suede	pelle scamosciata *__pel__-lay ska-mo-__sha__-ta*
terylene	terital *__te__-ree-tal*
velvet	velluto *vel-__loo__-toh*
wool	lana *__la__-na*

ACCESSORIES

bracelet	braccialetto *bra-cha-__let__-toh*
belt	cintura *cheen-__too__-ra*
brooch	spilla *__speel__-la*
button	bottone *bot-__toh__-nay*
earrings	orecchini *o-rek-__kee__-nee*
handbag	borsa *__bor__-sa*
handkerchief	fazzoletto *fat-soh-__let__-toh*
necklace	collana *kol-__la__-na*
pendant	ciondolo *__chon__-do-loh*
purse (U.K.)	borsellino *bor-sel-__lee__-noh*
(U.S.)	borsa *__bor__-sa*
ring	anello *a-__nel__-loh*
scarf	sciarpa *__shar__-pa*
umbrella	ombrello *om-__brel__-loh*
wallet	portafoglio *por-ta-__fol__-yoh*
watch	orologio *oh-roh-__lo__-joh*
zip	chiusura lampo *kee-oo-__zoo__-ra __lam__-poh*

The Hairdresser

I'd like to make an appointment	– Vorrei un appuntamento
	*vor-**ray**-ee oon ap-poon-ta-**men**-toh*
I want	– **a cut**
Desidero	il taglio
*day-**zee**-de-roh*	*eel **tal**-yoh*
	– **a trim**
	una spuntata
	*oo-na spoon-**ta**-ta*
	– **a blow-dry**
	asciugarli col phon
	*a-shoo-**gar**-lee kol fon*
I want my hair	– **fairly short**
Voglio i capelli	tagliati corti
***vol**-yoh ee ka-**payl**-lee*	*tal-**ya**-tee **kor**-tee*
	– **not too short**
	non troppo corti
	*non **trop**-poh **kor**-tee*
	– **short and curly**
	corti e ricci
	***kor**-tee ay **ree**-chee*
	– **layered**
	a ciocche
	*a **chok**-kay*
	– **in a fringe**
	con la frangia
	*kon la **fran**-ja*
Take more off	– **the front**
Tagliate più corti	davanti
*tal-**ya**-tay pee-yoo **kor**-tee*	*da-**van**-tee*
	– **the back**
	dietro
	dee-e-troh
Not too much off	– **the sides**
Non tagliate troppo	ai lati
*non tal-**ya**-tay **trop**-poh*	*a-ee **la**-tee*
	– **the top**
	sopra
	***so**-pra*

The Hairdresser

I'd like –	**a perm (permanent)**
Vorrei	la permanente
*vor-**ray**-ee*	*la payr-ma-**nen**-tay*
–	**a light perm**
	una permanente leggera
	*oo-na payr-ma-**nen**-tay led-**jay**-ra*
–	**a curly perm**
	una permanente riccia
	*oo-na payr-ma-**nen**-tay **ree**-cha*
–	**a shampoo and set**
	uno shampoo e messa in piega
	*oo-noh **sham**-poh e **mes**-sa een pee-**ay**-ga*
–	**my hair tinted**
	farmi la tintura
	*far-mee la teen-**too**-ra*
–	**my hair streaked**
	farmi le mesh
	far-mee lay mesh
The water is too hot –	L'acqua è troppo calda
	*lak-wa e **trop**-poh **kal**-da*
The dryer is too hot –	Il casco è troppo caldo
	*eel **ka**-skoh e **trop**-poh **kal**-doh*
I'd like –	**a conditioner**
Vorrei	un balsamo
*vor-**ray**-ee*	*oon **bal**-sa-moh*
–	**hair lacquer**
	la lacca
	*la **lak**-ka*
That's fine, thank you –	Va bene, grazie
	*va **be**-nay, **grat**-see-ay*

Dry Cleaners & Laundry

A dry-cleaner's is called a *lavasecco*; sometimes it is combined with *una lavanderia* or laundry which will usually provide a fairly quick service. You may also find a *lavanderia automatica*, a launderette, though they are few and far between, and even there you will often find staff who will wash the clothes for you.

Will you – **clean this skirt?**
Può smacchiare questa gonna?
pwoh *smak-kee-ah-ray kwes-ta gon-na?*

     – **press these trousers?**
stirare questi pantaloni?
stee-rah-ray kwes-tee pan-ta-loh-nee?

     – **wash and iron these shirts?**
lavare e stirare queste camicie?
la-vah-ray ay stee-rah-ray kwes-tay kam-ee-chay?

     – **wash these clothes?**
lavare questi vestiti?
la-vah-ray kwes-tee ves-tee-tee?

This stain is – **grease**
Questa è una macchia di unto
kwes-ta e oo-na mak-kee-a dee *oon-toh*

     – **blood**
sangue
san-gway

     – **coffee**
caffè
kaf-fe

This fabric is delicate – Questa stoffa è delicata
kwes-ta stof-fa e de-lee-ka-ta

When will my things be ready? – Quando saranno pronte le mie cose?
kwan-doh sa-ran-noh pron-tay lay mee-ay koh-say?

Is there a launderette nearby? – C'è una lavanderia automatica qui vicino?
che oo-na la-van-day-ree-a ow-toh-ma-tee-ka kwee vee-chee-noh?

There is something wrong with my camera – C'è qualche cosa che non va nella mia macchina fotografica
che kwal-kay koh-sa kay non va nel-la mee-a ma-kee-na foh-toh-gra-fee-ka

This is – **broken**
Questo è   rotto
kwes-toh e   *rot-toh*

  – **damaged**
danneggiato
dan-ned-ja-toh

  – **torn**
strappato
strap-pa-toh

Would you have a look at this please? – Può dare un'occhiata a questo per favore?
pwoh dah-ray oon ok-kee-a-ta a kwes-toh payr fa-voh-ray?

Can you fix it? – Può ripararlo?
pwoh ree-pa-rar-loh?

Can you reheel these shoes? – Può rifare i tacchi a queste scarpe?
pwoh ree-fah-ray ee tak-kee a kwes-tay skar-pay?

Have you got a replacement part? – Ha un pezzo di ricambio?
a oon pet-soh dee ree-kam-bee-oh?

When will it be ready? – Quando sarà pronto?
kwan-doh sa-ra pron-toh?

Can you do it quickly? – Può farlo in poco tempo?
pwoh far-loh een poh-koh tem-poh?

Can you give me – **some strong glue?**
Può darmi   della colla forte?
pwoh dar-mee   *del-la kol-la for-tay?*

  – **some string?**
della corda?
del-la kor-da?

  – **a needle and thread?**
un ago e del filo?
oon a-go ay del fee-loh?

The Bank

Banks are usually open from 8.30 a.m. until 1.30 p.m. Monday to Friday. If you present them with a traveller's cheque or Euro-cheque card they don't recognise, you will have to wait while they check it against their specimens. You may be told to pick up your currency from a different desk or *cassa*. You can also change money at hotels, large stores and, of course, *uffici di cambio*, but the rate of exchange tends to be less favourable. This is also true of regional banks, *Casse di Risparmio*. Offices at airports and major railway stations stay open at night and at weekends.

Will you change Potete cambiare *po-**tay**-tay kam-bee-**ah**-ray*	– **these traveller's cheques?** questi traveller's cheque? ***kwes**-tee **tre**-vuh-luhrz shek?*
	– **these notes (bills)?** questi biglietti? ***kwes**-tee beel-**yet**-tee?*
What is the rate for Quanto è il cambio per ***kwan**-toh e eel **kam**-bee-oh payr*	– **sterling?** la sterlina? *la stayr-**lee**-na?*
	– **dollars?** il dollaro? *eel **dol**-la-roh?*
I would like to cash a cheque with my Eurocheque card	– Vorrei riscuotere uno cheque con la mia carta Eurocheque *vor-**ray**-ee ree-**skwo**-tuh-ray **oo**-no shek kon la **mee**-a **kar**-ta ay-**oo**-roh-shek*
I would like to obtain a cash advance with my credit card	– Vorrei ottenere un anticipo con la mia carta di credito *vor-**ray**-ee ot-te-**nay**-ray oon an-**tee**-chee-poh kon la **mee**-a **kar**-ta dee **kre**-dee-toh*
Can you contact my bank to arrange for a transfer please?	– Può mettersi in contatto con la mia banca per organizzare un trasferimento di denaro? *pwoh **met**-ter-see een kon-**tat**-toh kon la **mee**-a **ban**-ka payr or-ga-**neet**-sah-ray oon tras-fe-ree-**men**-toh dee day-**nah**-roh?*

The Post Office

A large Italian post office can be rather confusing with a long row of desks, each providing a specific service. The ones you are most likely to need are those dealing with stamps – *francobolli* – and parcels – *pacchi*. If you just want stamps it's simpler to get them from a *tabacchino* or a bar with a tobacco counter.

How much is a letter – **to Britain?**
Quanto costa una lettera   per la Gran Bretagna?
***kwan*-toh *kos*-ta *oo*-na *let*-te-ra**   *payr la gran bre-**tan**-ya?*

     – **to the United States?**
     per gli Stati Uniti?
     *payr lyee **sta**-tee oo-**nee**-tee?*

Six 170 lire stamps, please – Sei francobolli da centosettanta lire per favore
     ***say*-ee fran-ko-**bol**-lee da chen-toh-set-**tan**-ta lee*-ray payr fa-**voh**-ray*

Can I have six stamps for – Posso avere sei francobolli per
postcards to Britain?   cartoline per la Gran Bretagna?
     ***pos*-soh a-**vay**-ray *say*-ee fran-ko-**bol**-lee payr kar-toh-**lee**-nay payr la gran bre-**tan**-ya?*

I want to send this parcel – Voglio spedire questo pacco
     ***vol*-yoh spe-**dee**-ray *kwes*-toh **pak**-koh*

I want to send a telegram – Voglio mandare un telegramma
     ***vol*-yoh man-**dah**-ray oon te-le-**gram**-ma*

Can I have a telegram form – Posso avere un modulo per un
please?   telegramma per favore?
     ***pos*-soh a-**vay**-ray oon **mo**-doo-loh payr oon te-le-**gram**-ma payr fa-**voh**-ray?*

When will it arrive? – Quando arriverà?
     ***kwan*-doh ar-ree-ve-**ra**?*

I want to send this by – Voglio mandare questo per
registered mail   raccomandata
     ***vol*-yoh man-**dah**-ray *kwes*-toh payr rak-koh-man-**da**-ta*

Using The Telephone

The simplest, but most expensive, way to telephone is from your hotel. Otherwise you can go to the local telephone centre (S.I.P.) or use a street telephone or one in a bar. The S.I.P is the best idea for a call home or for long distances – give the clerk the number you want and she will direct you to a booth. For other public phones you will need telephone tokens (one for a local call, eight or more for long distances). You insert these before dialling. In Italian, telephone numbers are not given as single digits, but in pairs, so that 4321 would be forty-three, twenty-one. You'll find numbers on page 110 and the telephone alphabet on page 114.

I would like to make a phone call to Britain	Voglio fare una telefonata in Gran Bretagna *vol-yoh **fah**-ray oo-na te-le-foh-**na**-ta een gran bre-**tan**-ya*
Can you get me this number?	Può farmi questo numero? *pwoh **far**-mee **kwes**-toh **noo**-may-roh?*
I wish to make a reversed charge (collect) call	Voglio addebitare la spesa al ricevente *vol-yoh ad-de-bee-**tah**-ray la **spay**-za al ree-chay-**ven**-tay*
I wish to make a person to person call to Signor Mario Rossi	Voglio fare una telefonata personale al Signor Mario Rossi *vol-yoh **fah**-ray oo-na tel-le-foh-**na**-ta payr-so-**na**-lay al **seen**-yor **mah**-ree-oh **ros**-see*
Which box do I use?	Quale cabina devo usare? ***kwa**-lay ka-**bee**-na **day**-voh oo-**zah**-ray?*
May I use the telephone please?	Posso usare il telefono per favore? ***pos**-soh oo-**zoh**-ray eel te-**le**-foh-noh payr fa-**voh**-ray?*
Do I need a token?	Ho bisogno di un gettone? *oh bee-**zon**-yoh dee oon jet-**toh**-nay?*
Can I have 8 tokens please?	Posso avere otto gettoni per favore? ***pos**-soh a-**vay**-ray ot-toh jet-**toh**-nee payr fa-**voh**-ray?*

Using the Telephone

Can I speak to Signor Rossi? – Posso parlare col signor Rossi?
pos-soh par-lah-ray kol seen-yor ros-see?

We have been cut off – Ci è stata tolta la comunicazione
*chee a sta-ta tol-ta la
ko-moo-nee-kat-see-oh-nay*

You may hear somebody at the other end of the line telling you:

Pronto – Hello
pron-toh

Le passo il signor Rossi – I'm putting you through to Signor
lay pas-soh eel seen-yor ros-see Rossi

Resti in linea – Hold the line
res-tee een lee-nay-a

Sto cercando di mettervi in – I am trying to connect you
comunicazione
*stoh cher-kan-doh dee met-ter-vee
een ko-moo-nee-kat-see-oh-nay*

La linea è occupata – The line is engaged (busy)
la lee-nay-a e ok-koo-pa-ta

Questo numero non risponde – There is no reply
*kwes-toh noo-may-roh non
ree-spon-day*

Non potete fare questo – This number cannot be obtained from
numero da questo this telephone
apparecchio
*non po-tay-tay fah-ray kwes-toh
noo-may-roh da kwes-toh
ap-pa-rek-kee-oh*

Non riesco a mettervi in – I cannot obtain this number
comunicazione
*non ree-e-skoh a met-ter-vee een
ko-moo-nee-kat-see-oh-nay*

Siete in linea – potete parlare – Please go ahead
*see-ay-tay een lee-nay-a –
po-tay-tay par-lah-ray*

Accidents

If a visit to a doctor is necessary, you will probably have to pay on the spot. Some of the cost of medical treatment is repayable under reciprocal EEC agreements for British and Irish visitors (form E111 should be obtained before departure), but proper accident and medical insurance is still advisable. Ambulances, which also have to be paid for, can be called by dialling 113.

There has been an accident	C'è stato un incidente *che **sta**-toh oon een-chee-**den**-tay*
Call an ambulance	Chiamate un'ambulanza *kee-a-**ma**-tay oon am-boo-**lant**-sa*
Get a doctor	Chiamate un medico *kee-a-**ma**-tay oon **me**-dee-koh*
He is unconscious	Ha perso conoscenza *a **payr**-soh ko-no-**shent**-sa*
She has been seriously injured	È ferita gravemente *e fe-**ree**-ta gra-vay-**men**-tay*
He has been badly hurt	Si è fatto molto male *see a **fat**-toh **mol**-toh **ma**-lay*
Can I have an appointment with the doctor?	Posso avere un appuntamento col medico? ***pos**-soh a-**vay**-ray oon ap-poon-ta-**men**-toh kol **me**-dee-koh?*
I have cut myself	Mi sono tagliato *mee **soh**-noh tal-**ya**-toh*
He has burnt himself	Si è bruciato *see e broo-**cha**-toh*
She has a temperature	Lei ha la febbre ***lay**-ee a la **feb**-bray*
I have hurt Mi sono fatto male ad *mee **soh**-noh **fat**-toh **ma**-lay ad*	**my arm** un braccio *oon **bra**-choh*
	my leg una gamba *oo-na **gam**-ba*

Accidents

I have had a fall –	Sono caduto *soh-noh ka-doo-toh*
He has been bitten –	È stato morso *e sta-toh mor-soh*
She has been stung –	È stata punta *e sta-ta poon-ta*
I have broken my arm –	Mi sono rotto il braccio *mee soh-noh rot-toh eel bra-cho*
He has dislocated his shoulder –	Si è slogato una spalla *see e slo-ga-toh oo-na spal-la*
She has sprained her ankle –	Ha preso una storta alla caviglia *a pray-zoh oo-na stor-ta al-la ka-veel-ya*
I have pulled a muscle –	Ho uno stiramento *oh oo-noh stee-ra-men-toh*
There is a swelling here –	C'è un gonfio qui *che oon gon-fee-oh kwee*
It is inflamed here –	È infiammato qui *e een-fee-am-ma-toh kwee*
It is painful Fa male *fa ma-lay*	– **to walk** a camminare *a kam-mee-nah-ray*
	– **to swallow** ad inghiottire *ad een-gee-ot-tee-ray*
	– **to breathe** a respirare *a re-spee-rah-ray*
Will I have to go into hospital? –	Devo andare in ospedale? *day-voh an-dah-ray een o-spe-da-lay?*
Will an operation be necessary? –	C'è bisogno di un intervento? *che bee-zon-yoh dee oon een-ter-ven-toh?*
How do I get reimbursed? –	Come posso essere rimborsato? *koh-may pos-soh es-se-ray reem-bor-sa-toh?*

Symptoms

I have – Ho *oh*	**a headache** un mal di testa *oon mal dee **tes**-ta*
	– an earache un mal d'orecchi *oon mal do-**rek**-kee*
	– a sore throat un mal di gola *oon mal dee **goh**-la*
I can't sleep –	Non riesco a dormire *non ree-**es**-koh a dor-**mee**-ray*
I have sunstroke –	Ho preso un'insolazione *oh **pray**-zoh oon een-soh-lat-see-**oh**-nay*
My tongue is coated –	Ho la lingua patinosa *oh la **leen**-gwa pa-tee-**noh**-za*
My stomach is upset –	Ho dei disturbi di stomaco *oh **day**-ee dees-**toor**-bee dee **sto**-ma-koh*
I feel nauseous (nauseated) –	Ho la nausea *oh la **now**-zay-a*
I think I have food poisoning –	Penso di essere intossicato dal cibo ***pen**-soh dee **es**-se-ray een-tos-see-**ka**-toh dal **chee**-boh*
I have been sick –	Ho vomitato *oh vo-mee-**ta**-toh*
I have diarrhoea –	Ho la diarrea *oh la dee-ar-**ray**-a*
I am constipated –	Sono stitico ***soh**-noh **stee**-tee-koh*
I feel faint –	Mi sento svenire *mee **sen**-toh sve-**nee**-ray*
Must I stay in bed? –	Devo stare a letto? ***day**-voh **stah**-ray a **let**-toh?*
Will I be able to go out tomorrow? –	Posso uscire domani? ***pos**-soh oo-**shee**-ray do-**ma**-nee?*

Conditions

I am allergic to penicillin – Sono allergico alla penicillina
*soh-noh al-**ler**-jee-koh **al**-la
pe-nee-cheel-**lee**-na*

I have high blood pressure – Ho la pressione alta
*oh la pres-see-**oh**-nay **al**-ta*

I am a diabetic – Sono diabetico
*soh-noh dee-a-**be**-tee-koh*

I am taking these drugs – Sto prendendo queste medicine
*stoh pren-**den**-doh **kwes**-tay
me-dee-**chee**-nay*

Can you give me an Italian prescription for them? – Può farmi una ricetta italiana per questa medicina?
*pwoh **far**-mee oo-na ree-**chet**-ta
ee-ta-lee-**a**-na payr **kwes**-ta
me-dee-**chee**-na?*

I am pregnant – Sono incinta
*soh-noh een-**cheen**-ta*

I am on the pill – Sto prendendo la pillola
*stoh pren-**den**-doh la **peel**-loh-la*

My blood group is . . . – Il mio gruppo sanguigno è . . .
*eel **mee**-oh **groop**-poh san-**gween**-yoh e . . .*

I don't know my blood group – Non conosco il mio gruppo sanguigno
*non ko-**noh**-skoh eel **mee**-oh **groop**-poh
san-**gween**-yoh*

Parts of the Body

ankle	caviglia *ka-veel-ya*	**kidney**	rene *ray-nay*
arm	braccio *bra-choh*	**knee**	ginocchio *jee-nok-kee-oh*
back	schiena *skee-ay-na*	**leg**	gamba *gam-ba*
blood	sangue *san-gway*	**lip**	labbro *lab-broh*
bone	osso *os-soh*	**liver**	fegato *fe-ga-toh*
breast	petto *pet-toh*	**lungs**	polmoni *pol-moh-nee*
cheek	guancia *gwan-cha*	**mouth**	bocca *bok-ka*
chest	torace *to-ra-chay*	**muscle**	muscolo *moos-ko-loh*
chin	mento *men-toh*	**neck**	collo *kol-loh*
ear	orecchio *o-rek-kee-oh*	**nose**	naso *na-zoh*
elbow	gomito *go-mee-toh*	**shin**	stinco *steen-koh*
eye	occhio *ok-kee-oh*	**shoulder**	spalla *spal-la*
face	viso *vee-zoh*	**skin**	pelle *pel-lay*
finger	dito *dee-toh*	**spine**	spina *spee-na*
foot	piede *pee-ay-day*	**stomach**	stomaco *sto-ma-koh*
hair	capelli *ka-payl-lee*	**throat**	gola *goh-la*
hand	mano *ma-noh*	**thumb**	pollice *pol-lee-chay*
head	testa *tes-ta*	**tooth**	dente *den-tay*
heart	cuore *kwoh-ray*	**wrist**	polso *pol-soh*

The Dentist

I need to see the dentist – Devo vedere il dentista
day-voh ve-day-ray eel den-tee-sta

I have a toothache – Ho mal di denti
oh mal dee den-tee

It's this one – È questo
e kwes-toh

I've broken a tooth – Mi sono spezzato un dente
mee soh-noh spet-sa-toh oon den-tay

The filling has come out – È uscita l'otturazione
e oo-shee-ta lot-too-rat-see-oh-nay

Will you have to take it out? – Bisogna toglierlo?
bee-zon-ya tol-yer-loh?

Are you going to fill it? – Farà un'otturazione?
fa-ra oo-not-too-rat-see-oh-nay?

That hurt – M'ha fatto male
ma fat-toh ma-lay

Please give me an injection – Mi faccia un'iniezione per favore
mee fa-cha oo-neen-yet-see-oh-nay payr fa-voh-ray

My gums hurt – Mi fanno male le gengive
mee fan-noh ma-lay lay jen-jee-vay

My false teeth are broken – La mia dentiera si è rotta
la mee-a den-tee-e-ra see e rot-ta

Can you repair them? – Può ripararla?
pwoh ree-pa-rar-la?

The Time

What time is it?	– Che ore sono? *kay **oh**-ray **soh**-noh?*	
It is ...	– Sono ... *soh-noh*	
10 o'clock	– le dieci *lay dee-**ay**-chee*	
5 past 10		e cinque *ay **cheen**-kway*
10 past 10		e dieci *ay dee-**ay**-chee*
A quarter past 10	– le dieci *lay dee-**ay**-chee*	e un quarto *ay oon **kwar**-toh*
20 past 10		e venti *ay **ven**-tee*
25 past 10		e venticinque *ay ven-tee-**cheen**-kway*
half past 10		e mezza *ay **med**-za*
25 to 11		meno venticinque ***may**-noh ven-tee-**cheen**-kway*
20 to 11		meno venti ***may**-noh **ven**-tee*
a quarter to 11	– le undici *lay **oon**-dee-chee*	meno un quarto ***may**-noh oon **kwar**-toh*
10 to 11		meno dieci ***may**-noh dee-**ay**-chee*
5 to 11		meno cinque ***may**-noh **cheen**-kway*
11 o'clock	– le undici *lay **oon**-dee-chee*	

The Time

A few of these expressions may be useful

tonight – stasera
sta-say-ra

at night – di notte
dee not-tay

the morning – la mattina
la mat-tee-na

this afternoon – questo pomeriggio
kwes-toh po-may-reed-joh

at midday – a mezzogiorno
a med-zoh-jor-noh

before midnight – prima di mezzanotte
pree-ma dee med-za-not-tay

after 3 o'clock – dopo le tre
do-poh lay tray

at half past 6 – alle sei e mezza
al-lay say-ee ay med-za

nearly 5 o'clock – quasi le cinque
kwah-zee lay cheen-kway

at about 1 o'clock – circa l'una
cheer-ka loo-na

in an hour's time – fra un'ora
fra oo-noh-ra

two hours ago – due ore fa
doo-ay oh-ray fa

in half an hour – fra mezz'ora
fra med-zoh-ra

soon – fra poco
fra poh-koh

early – presto
pres-toh

late – tardi
tar-dee

Numbers
Up to a million

0	zero *tsay-roh*	19	diciannove *dee-chan-**no**-vay*
1	uno, una ***oo**-noh, **oo**-na*	20	venti ***ven**-tee*
2	due ***doo**-ay*	21	ventuno *ven-**too**-noh*
3	tre *tray*	22	ventidue *ven-tee-**doo**-ay*
4	quattro ***kwat**-troh*	23	ventitre *ven-tee-**tray***
5	cinque ***cheen**-kway*	30	trenta ***tren**-ta*
6	sei ***say**-ee*	40	quaranta *kwa-**ran**-ta*
7	sette ***set**-tay*	50	cinquanta *cheen-**kwan**-ta*
8	otto ***ot**-toh*	60	sessanta *ses-**san**-ta*
9	nove ***no**-vay*	70	settanta *set-**tan**-ta*
10	dieci *dee-**ay**-chee*	80	ottanta *ot-**tan**-ta*
11	undici ***oon**-dee-chee*	90	novanta *noh-**van**-ta*
12	dodici ***doh**-dee-chee*	100	cento ***chen**-toh*
13	tredici ***tray**-dee-chee*	110	centodieci *chen-toh-dee-**ay**-chee*
14	quattordici *kwat-**tor**-dee-chee*	200	duecento *doo-ay-**chen**-toh*
15	quindici ***kween**-dee-chee*	300	trecento *tray-**chen**-toh*
16	sedici ***say**-dee-chee*	1,000	mille ***meel**-lay*
17	diciassette *dee-chas-**set**-tay*	2,000	duemila *doo-ay-**mee**-la*
18	diciotto *dee-**chot**-toh*	1,000,000	un milione *oon meel-**yoh**-nay*

Numbers
The First to the Last

1st	primo *pree-moh*	16th	sedicesimo *say-dee-che-zee-moh*
2nd	secondo *se-kon-doh*	17th	diciassettesimo *dee-chas-set-te-zee-moh*
3rd	terzo *tert-soh*	18th	diciottesimo *dee-chot-te-zee-moh*
4th	quarto *kwar-toh*	19th	diciannovesimo *dee-chan-noh-ve-zee-moh*
5th	quinto *kween-toh*	20th	ventesimo *ven-te-zee-moh*
6th	sesto *ses-toh*	21st	ventunesimo *ven-too-ne-zee-moh*
7th	settimo *set-tee-moh*	22nd	ventiduesimo *ven-tee-doo-e-zee-moh*
8th	ottavo *ot-ta-voh*	23rd	ventitreesimo *ven-tee-tray-e-zee-moh*
9th	nono *no-noh*		
10th	decimo *de-chee-moh*	30th	trentesimo *tren-te-zee-moh*
11th	undicesimo *oon-dee-che-zee-moh*	40th	quarantesimo *kwa-ran-te-zee-moh*
12th	dodicesimo *doh-dee-che-zee-moh*	50th	cinquantesimo *cheen-kwan-te-zee-moh*
13th	tredicesimo *tray-dee-che-zee-moh*		
14th	quattordicesimo *kwat-tor-dee-che-zee-moh*	100th	centesimo *chen-te-zee-moh*
15th	quindicesimo *kween-dee-che-zee-moh*	1,000th	millesimo *meel-le-zee-moh*

a half	la metà *la may-ta*	a dozen	una dozzina *oo-na dot-see-na*
a quarter	un quarto *oon kwar-toh*	half a dozen	una mezza dozzina *oo-na med-za dot-see-na*
a third	un terzo *oon tert-soh*	5 times	cinque volte *cheen-kway vol-tay*
10%	dieci per cento *dee-ay-chee payr chen-toh*	the last (one)	l'ultimo *lool-tee-moh*

The Calendar

Sunday	domenica *doh-**may**-nee-ka*	**January**	gennaio *jen-**na**-yoh*
Monday	lunedì *loo-nay-**dee***	**February**	febbraio *feb-**bra**-yoh*
Tuesday	martedì *mar-tay-**dee***	**March**	marzo ***mart**-soh*
Wednesday	mercoledì *mer-ko-lay-**dee***	**April**	aprile *a-**pree**-lay*
Thursday	giovedì *joh-vay-**dee***	**May**	maggio ***mad**-joh*
Friday	venerdì *ve-ner-**dee***	**June**	giugno ***joon**-yoh*
Saturday	sabato ***sa**-ba-toh*	**July**	luglio ***lool**-yoh*
on Friday	venerdì *ve-ner-**dee***	**August**	agosto *a-**gos**-toh*
next Tuesday	martedì prossimo *mar-tay-**dee** **pros**-see-moh*	**September**	settembre *set-**tem**-bray*
yesterday	ieri ***ye**-ree*	**October**	ottobre *ot-**toh**-bray*
today	oggi ***od**-jee*	**November**	novembre *no-**vem**-bray*
tomorrow	domani *do-**ma**-nee*	**December**	dicembre *dee-**chem**-bray*
spring	la primavera *la pree-ma-**vay**-ra*	**in June**	in giugno *een **joon**-yoh*
summer	l'estate *lay-**sta**-tay*	**July 6th**	il sei luglio *eel **say**-ee **lool**-yoh*
autumn (fall)	l'autunno *low-**toon**-noh*	**next week**	la settimana prossima *la set-tee-**ma**-na **pros**-see-ma*
winter	l'inverno *leen-**ver**-noh*	**last month**	il mese scorso *eel **may**-zay **skohr**-soh*
in spring	in primavera *een pree-ma-**vay**-ray*		
in summer	d'estate *day-**sta**-tay*		

New Year's Day	January 1st
Easter Monday	
Liberation Day	April 25th
Labour Day	May 1st
Feast of the Assumption	August 15th
All Saint's Day	November 1st
Feast of the Immaculate Conception	December 8th
Christmas Day	December 25th
St Stephen's Day	December 26th

Besides the national holidays, it's also worth knowing the approximate dates of some of Italy's many local festivals.

Assisi	*Calendimaggio*, the spring festival, held in early May
Asti	*Il Palio*, held in late September
Florence	*Il Gioco del Calcio*, a lively commemoration of a sixteenth-century football match, held in late June
Siena	*Il Palio*, possibly the most famous of them all, the pageant followed by the horse race in the city square, July 2nd and August 16th
Venice	*La Regatta*, September 2nd
Viareggio	*Il Carnevale*, held on the days just preceding the start of Lent, generally mid-February

The Alphabet

A	come	**Ancona**		N	come	**Napoli**	
a	*koh-may*	*an-koh-na*		*en-ne*	*koh-may*	*na-poh-lee*	
B	for	**Bari**		O	for	**Otranto**	
bee		*bah-ree*		*o*		*o-tran-toh*	
C		**Catania**		P		**Palermo**	
chee		*ka-ta-nee-a*		*pee*		*pa-ler-moh*	
D		**Domodossola**		Q		**quarto**	
dee		*do-mo-dos-so-la*		*koo*		*kwar-toh*	
E		**Empoli**		R		**Roma**	
ay		*em-po-lee*		*er-re*		*roh-ma*	
F		**Firenze**		S		**Savona**	
ef-fe		*fee-rent-say*		*es-se*		*sa-voh-na*	
G		**Genova**		T		**Torino**	
jee		*je-noh-va*		*tee*		*to-ree-noh*	
H		**Hotel**		U		**Udine**	
ak-ka		*oh-tel*		*oo*		*oo-dee-nay*	
I		**Imperia**		V		**Venezia**	
ee		*eem-pay-ree-a*		*voo*		*ve-nayt-see-a*	
J				W			
ee loon-goh						*dop-pee-oh-voo*	
K				X			
kap-pa						*eex*	
L		**Livorno**		Y			
el-le		*lee-vor-noh*		*ee gre-koh*			
M		**Milano**		Z			
em-me		*mee-la-noh*		*tsay-ta*			

Abbreviations

ACI	Automobile Club d'Italia (*Italian Motoring Organization*)
CEE	Comunità Economica Europea (*the Common Market*)
CIT	Compagnia Italiana del Turismo } *Italian Tourist*
ENIT	Ente Nazionale Italiano per il Turismo } *Authorities*
FS	Ferrovie dello Stato (*Italian Railways*)
IVA	Imposta sul Valore Aggiunto (*VAT, purchase tax*)
PT	Poste e Telecomunicazioni (*Post Office*)
RAI	Radio Audizioni Italiane (*Italian Radio and Television*)
SIP	Società Italiana per l'esercizio telefonico (*Italian Telephone Company*)
TCI	Touring Club Italiano (*Italian Touring Club*)

Descriptions

First of all, a list of colours:

beige	beige *bej*	**mauve**	malva *mal-va*
black	nero *nay-roh*	**orange**	arancione *a-ran-choh-nay*
blue	blu *bloo*	**pink**	rosa *roh-za*
brown	marrone *mar-roh-nay*	**purple**	viola *vee-oh-la*
cream	crema *kray-ma*	**red**	rosso *ros-soh*
fawn	fulvo *fool-voh*	**silver**	argento *ar-jen-toh*
gold	oro *o-roh*	**tan**	rossiccio *ros-see-choh*
green	verde *ver-day*	**white**	bianco *bee-an-ko*
grey	grigio *gree-joh*	**yellow**	giallo *jal-loh*

and a few other handy adjectives:

bad	cattivo *kat-tee-voh*	**interesting**	interessante *in-te-res-san-tay*
beautiful	bello *bel-loh*	**little**	piccolo *pee-kol-loh*
big	grande *gran-day*	**long**	lungo *loon-goh*
cold	freddo *fred-doh*	**new**	nuovo *nwoh-voh*
dear	caro *ka-roh*	**old**	vecchio *vek-kyoh*
fast	veloce *ve-lo-chay*	**short**	corto *kor-toh*
good	buono *bwoh-noh*	**slow**	lento *len-toh*
hot	caldo *kal-doh*	**terrible**	terribile *ter-ree-bee-lay*

Conversion Tables

In the tables for weight and length, the central figure may be read as either a metric or an imperial measurement.

feet		metres		lb		kg
3.3	1	0.3		2.2	1	0.45
6.6	2	0.61		4.4	2	0.91
9.9	3	0.91		6.6	3	1.4
13.1	4	1.22		8.8	4	1.8
16.4	5	1.52		11	5	2.2
19.7	6	1.83		13.2	6	2.7
23	7	2.13		15.4	7	3.2
26.2	8	2.44		17.6	8	3.6
29.5	9	2.74		19.8	9	4.1
32.9	10	3.05		22	10	4.5

inches		cm
0.39	1	2.54
0.79	2	5.08
1.18	3	7.62
1.57	4	10.6
1.97	5	12.7
2.36	6	15.2
2.76	7	17.8
3.15	8	20.3
3.54	9	22.9
3.9	10	25.4
4.3	11	27.9
4.7	12	30.1

Exchange Rates

£1 =

$1 =

100 lire =
250 lire =
500 lire =
1,000 lire =
2,000 lire =
5,000 lire =
10,000 lire =
50,000 lire =

Conversion Tables

Kilometres	Miles	Centigrade	Fahrenheit
10	6.2	0	32
20	12.4	5	41
30	18.6	10	50
40	24.9	15	59
50	31	17	63
60	37.3	20	68
70	43.5	22	72
80	49.7	24	75
90	56	26	79
100	62	28	82
110	68.3	30	86
120	74.6	35	95
130	81	37	98.4
140	87	38	100
150	93.2	40	104
160	100	50	122
200	124	100	212
300	186		
500	310		

TYRE PRESSURES

lb/sq in	15	18	20	22	24	26	28	30	33	35
kg/sq cm	1.1	1.3	1.4	1.5	1.7	1.8	2	2.1	2.3	2.5

litres	UK gallons	US gallons	litres	UK gallons	US gallons
5	1.1	1.3	25	5.5	6.5
10	2.2	2.6	30	6.6	7.8
15	3.3	3.9	35	7.7	9.1
20	4.4	5.2	40	8.8	10.4

Place-names

Abruzzi e Molise	*a-**broot**-see ay **mo**-lee-zay*	Firenze (Florence)	*fee-**rent**-say*
Agrigento	*a-gree-**jen**-toh*	Fiumicino	*fee-oo-mee-**chee**-noh*
Alassio	*a-**las**-see-oh*	Forte dei Marmi	*for-tay day-ee **mar**-mee*
Amalfi	*a-**mal**-fee*		
Ancona	*an-**koh**-na*	Genova (Genoa)	*je-noh-va*
Anzio	*ant-see-oh*		
Arezzo	*a-**ret**-soh*	Gubbio	*goob-bee-oh*
Assisi	*as-**see**-zee*	Ischia	*ee-**skee**-a*
Bari	***bah**-ree*	L'Aquila	***lak**-wee-la*
Basilicata	*ba-zee-lee-**ka**-ta*	La Spezia	*la **spayt**-see-a*
Bergamo	*ber-**ga**-moh*	Lazio	***lat**-see-oh*
Bologna	*bo-**lon**-ya*	Lecce	***le**-chay*
Bordighera	*bor-dee-**ge**-ra*	Liguria	*lee-**goo**-ree-a*
Bracciano	*bra-**cha**-noh*	Livorno (Leghorn)	*lee-**vor**-noh*
Brescia	***bre**-sha*		
Brindisi	***breen**-dee-zee*	Lombardia	*lom-bar-**dee**-a*
Cagliari	***kal**-ya-ree*	Loreto	*lo-**ray**-toh*
Calabria	*ka-**la**-bree-a*	Lucca	***look**-ka*
Campania	*kam-**pan**-ya*	Mantova (Mantua)	***man**-to-va*
Capri	***ka**-pree*		
Catania	*ka-**tan**-ya*	Marche	***mar**-kay*
Civitavecchia	*chee-vee-ta-**vayk**-kee-a*	Messina	*mes-**see**-na*
		Milano (Milan)	*mee-**la**-noh*
Como	***ko**-moh*		
Cortina	*kor-**tee**-na*	Modena	***mo**-day-na*
Cosenza	*ko-**zent**-sa*	Montepulciano	*mon-tay-pool-**cha**-noh*
Cremona	*kray-**moh**-na*		
Elba	***el**-ba*	Napoli (Naples)	***na**-poh-lee*
Emilia-Romagna	*ay-**meel**-ya roh-**man**-ya*		
		Orvieto	*or-vee-**ay**-toh*
Ferrara	*fer-**rah**-ra*	Ostia Antica	*o-stee-a an-**tee**-ka*
Fiesole	*fee-**ay**-zoh-lay*	Padova (Padua)	***pa**-do-va*

Place-names

Palermo	*pa-**ler**-moh*	**Siena**	*see-**e**-na*
Parma	***par**-ma*	**Sorrento**	*sor-**ren**-toh*
Pavia	*pa-**vee**-a*	**Spoleto**	*spo-**lay**-toh*
Pescara	*pe-**ska**-ra*	**Stresa**	***stray**-za*
Perugia	*pe-**roo**-ja*	**Taormina**	*ta-or-**mee**-na*
Piemonte	*pee-e-**mon**-tay*	**Todi**	*to-dee*
Pisa	***pee**-za*	**Trentino-**	*trayn-**tee**-noh **al**-toh*
Pompei	*pom-**pe**-ee*	**Alto-Adige**	*a-dee-jay*
Portofino	*por-toh-**fee**-noh*	**Toscana**	*toh-**ska**-na*
Puglia	***pool**-ya*	**Trieste**	*tree-e-stay*
(Apulia)		**Torino**	*to-**ree**-noh*
Rapallo	*ra-**pal**-loh*	(Turin)	
Ravenna	*ra-**ven**-na*	**Umbria**	***oom**-bree-a*
Reggio	*red-joh ka-**la**-bree-a*	**Urbino**	*oor-**bee**-noh*
Calabria		**Valle d'Aosta**	*val-lay da-o-sta*
Rimini	***ree**-mee-nee*	**Veneto**	*ve-ne-toh*
Salerno	*sa-**ler**-noh*	**Venezia**	*ve-**nayt**-see-a*
San	*san jee-meen-**ya**-noh*	(Venice)	
Gimignano		**Verona**	*ve-**roh**-na*
Sardegna	*sar-**dayn**-ya*	**Viareggio**	*vee-a-**rayd**-joh*
(Sardinia)		**Vicenza**	*vee-**chent**-sa*
Sicilia (Sicily)	*see-**cheel**-ya*	**Volterra**	*vol-**ter**-ra*

Signs & Notices

Ai treni	– This way to the trains
Al completo	– Full
Alt	– Stop
Aperto	– Open
Ascensore	– Lift (elevator)
Attenzione – lavori in corso	– Danger – men at work
Avanti	– Cross now
Cassa (*in shop*)	– Pay here
(*in bank etc*)	– Counter
Chiuso	– Closed
Degustazione	– Sampling (*of wine, oysters etc*)
Donne	– Ladies
Fermata	– Bus stop
Guasto	– Out of order
Ingresso gratuito *or* **libero**	– No obligation to buy
Libero	– Vacant
Non toccare	– Do not touch
Occupato	– Engaged

Pericoloso sporgersi	–	Do not lean out
Polizia	–	Police
Saldi	–	Sale
Servizio compreso	–	Service included
Servizio escluso	–	Service not included
Signore	–	Ladies
Signori	–	Gentlemen
Si prega di attendere	–	Please wait
Sottopassaggio	–	Underpass
Spingere	–	Push
Suonare	–	Ring
Tirare	–	Pull
Uomini	–	Gentlemen
Uscita	–	Exit
Vernice fresca	–	Wet paint
Vietato il bagno	–	No bathing
Vietato calpestare le aiuole	–	Keep off the grass
Vietato fumare	–	No smoking

Index

accident	15, 102	brandy	72
activities	49	breakdown	34
address	25, 39	breakdown van	34
adhesive tape	82	breakfast	42
air-conditioning	43	breeze	54
air-mattress	51	broken	44, 97
airport	22	brush	47
allowance	18	bucket	51
ambulance	15, 102	building	58
amusement park	49	bus	24
arrive, to	23	bus tour	58
ashtray	43		
automatic (car)	33	camera	86
		camp, to	50
babysit, to	49	camp bed	51
back pack	51	camp chair	51
baggage=luggage		camp site	51
baggage room	27	can opener	47, 51
bandage	85	car	33, 34 etc
bank	98	car number	39
Baptist	53	car park	31
bath	41, 47	carafe	62
bathroom	47	caravan	50
beach	56	carry, to	19
bed	47	castle	22, 58
bedding	46	cathedral	58
beer	72	Catholic	53
bend	39	centre	22
bill	44, 63, 75	chair	47
blanket	43	change (money)	25, 75
blood group	105	change, to (buses etc)	24, 29
blow-out	39	change, to (clothes)	56
booking	46	charge	33, 74
bottle (for baby)	49	check, to	30
(of wine etc)	78	check=cheque	
bottle opener	47	cheque	98
brake	36, 39	child	48

church	53	departure board	28
cigar	83	deposit	75
cigarettes	83	dessert	62
cigarette lighter	83	detour	32
clean, to	96	dining car	29
close	38	dinner	42
close, to	13	disco	57
clothes	96	dislocate	103
coach=bus		distilled water	30
coat hanger	43	documents	33
coffee	72	door	46
cold	54, 115	double room	41
cold (in nose)	84	drinking water	50
colours	115	drive, to	33, 38
concert	57	driver's licence=driving	
connecting flight	18	licence	
connection (bad)	35	driving licence	18, 38
consulate	15	dry, to	17
contact, to	46		
conveyor belt	19	elevator	42
cooker	46	English-speaking	58
corkscrew	47	envelopes	82
cosmetics	85	equipment	57
cot	41, 48	excuse me	11
couchette	27	exhaust	35
credit card	75, 98		
crib	41, 48		
curve	39	fail (brakes)	39
		fall	103
		false teeth	107
damaged	97	fan belt	35
daughter	48	far	22
day	33	fare	24
dead battery	34	feed, to	48
deck chair	56	festival	57
declare, to	18	fill	30
delay	16	film (movie)	57
dentist	107	film (for camera)	86

Index

fine	38	hold-up	32
fire	15	hospital	103
fish	79	hot	44, 54, 115
fishing	57	hotel	42
fix, to	35, 47, 97	how long	16, 24
flashlight	51	how much	74
flat tyre	34	hurry	25
flush, to	47	hurt	49, 102
follow	14	husband	48
forget	16		
fork	47, 51	ignition key	35
frying pan	51	ill	49
fuse	36, 47	injured	102
		ink	82
garage	34	insurance company	15, 35
gas (for car)	34	iron, to	44
gas (in house)	47	itemized bill	35, 75
give way, to	38		
glass	62	key	43, 46
glue	97	kitchen	47, 52
golf	57	knife	47, 51
goodbye	10		
green card	38	last	24, 111
groceries	80	launderette	96
guide	58	lawyer	15
guide-book	58	leak	35, 47
guy line	51	leave, to	44
		left	25
hair	94	left luggage	27
hay fever	84	letter	99
headache	84	license number	39
heating	44, 46	lift	42
help, to	14	light	43
help (household)	46	litre	30, 78
high chair	49	lock	44
high tide	55	look for, to	12
highway	23	lose, to	15

lose, to (one's way)	17	outlet	43
lost	15	overheat, to	34
luggage	16, 19	overtake, to	39
luggage trolley	19		
lunch	42	paddling pool	49
		pail	51
mallet	51	pan	47
map	23, 82	pass	32
martini	72	pass, to (in car)	39
matches	51, 83	passport	18
meal	52, 63	parcel	99
meat	79	park, to	31
mechanic	34	parking disc	31
menu	60	parking lights	31
mileage	33	parking lot=car park	
mineral water	63	part (spare part)	35
minister	53	party	17
money	14, 75	pay, to	18, 75
mosque	53	pen	82
motorway	23	pencil	82
muddy	50	penknife	51
museum	58	petrol	34
		photo	59, 86
newspaper	82	pick up, to	27
night	41, 52	pillow	43
night club	57	pipe	83
no	10	pitch, to (tent)	50
no-smoking compartment	29	plastic bag	77
noisy	43	plate	47, 51
notepaper	43, 82	platform	28
number, car	39	play, to	57
		plug	44
one-way ticket	26	police	15
open	52	police station	15, 38
open, to	29	porter	19
operate, to	33	postcard	59, 82
organized	49	post office	22

Index

priest	53	shower	41, 50
private	56	sightseeing tour	58
Protestant	53	signal	38
public	58	signal, to	39
		single room	41
rabbi	53	single (ticket)	26
radiator	35	sink	47
rain, to	54	skid, to	39
razor	43	sleep, to	48, 104
receipt	75	sleeper	27
reduction	75	sleeping bag	51
refrigerator	47	smoking compartment	27
regulation	38	snow, to	54
rent, to	33, 46	socket	43
repeat	14	son	48
replacement	97	sore throat	84
reserve, to	41	sorry	10, 38, 49
restroom=toilet		souvenir	59
return (ticket)	26	speciality	61
reverse	33	speed limit	32
right	25	spill	17
river	58	spoon	47, 51
room	41	stain	96
round-trip ticket	26	stamp	99
route	23	stay, to	18, 41
rucksack	51	sting, to	103
run into, to	39	stop, to	25, 29, 38
		stove	46
safe	42	street map	82
sailing	56	string	97
salty	62	student	75
sandwich	73	suddenly	38
sea	55	suitcase	27
seat	26, 29	sunglasses	76
senior citizens	75	sunshade	56
sheet	47	sunstroke	104
sheet sleeping bag	52	surfing	56

Index

swerve, to	39	tyre	34, 37
swim, to	56	tyre pressure	30
swimming pool	56		
synagogue	53	vacuum cleaner	47
table	47	vegetables	81
tap	47	voltage	43
taxi	19		
tea	72	wait	25
telegram	99	walk	57
telephone	100	walk, to	22
temperature	54, 102	wallet	15
tennis	57	warm, to	49
tent	50	wash, to	96
thermos flask	51	wash, to (dishes)	51
thunderstorm	55	wash basin	44, 47
ticket	24, 29, 57	washroom	51
tie-up	32	water	63
tire=tyre		water heater	46
toilet	22, 47	water-skiing	56
toilet paper	44	way (the way to . . .)	22
toiletries	85	weather	54
toll	32	wet	39
tooth	107	what time	13, 29
toothache	84	where	22
torch	51	wife	48
torn	97	window	44, 47
tour	58	windscreen	30
Tourist Information Office	12, 23	windscreen washer	30
tow	34	windshield	30
tow-truck	34	windy	54
towel	43	wine	62, 72
town guide	58	wine list	62
trailer	50	wrong (something wrong)	34, 97
train	28		
traveller's cheques	44, 75, 98	yes	10
trouble	34	yield, to	38
turn, to	25	youth hostel	52

Personal Details

Name
Nome

Home address
Indirizzo

Tel

Address in Italy
Indirizzo in Italia

Tel

In case of accident notify
In caso d'incidente avvisare

Tel

Passport No
No di passaporto

Car No
No d'immatriculazione

Blood group
Gruppo sanguigno

HALT sign

 All Vehicles Prohibited

 STOP Customs

 No Parking I on even days II on odd days

 Use of Horn Prohibited

 Speed Limit

 DANGER

 Tunnel

 Loose Chippings

 Slippery Road

 Cross Roads with minor road

Cross Winds

 PRIORITY ROAD

 END of priority. Give way to traffic from right.

  DANGER Give way to traffic from right. (France)

 PRIORITY ROAD.

 Level Crossing

 Minimum Speed Limit

 END of Minimum Speed

 Keep Right

 Switch on headlights

 Snow Chains or Tyres Compulsory

 Cycle path Compulsory

 First Aid

 First Aid

 Information

 Subway or Bridge

 Pedestrian Crossing

 Mechanical Help

 Filling Station